The
Garland Library
of
War and Peace

The
Garland Library
of
War and Peace

Under the General Editorship of

Blanche Wiesen Cook, *John Jay College, C.U.N.Y.*

Sandi E. Cooper, *Richmond College, C.U.N.Y.*

Charles Chatfield, *Wittenberg University*

Militarism and Anti-Militarism

With Special Regard
to the International
Young Socialist Movement

by
Karl Liebknecht

translated, with a preface, by
Alexander Sirnis

with a new introduction
for the Garland Edition by
Marian A. Low

Garland Publishing, Inc., New York & London
1973

WITHDRAWN

Library of Congress Cataloging in Publication Data

Liebknecht, Karl Paul August Friedrich, 1871-1919.
   Militarism and anti-militarism.

   (Garland library of war and peace)
   Reprint of the 1917 ed. published by Socialist
Labour Press, Glasgow.
   Includes bibliographical references.
   1. Militarism. I. Title. II. Series.
JX1952.L613 1973   355.021'3   76-147521
ISBN 0-8240-0309-8

Introduction

The heroic, lonely, idiosyncratic figure of Karl Liebknecht emerged as an international symbol of vociferous antimilitarism prior to World War I; that war raised him to an internationally revered, almost legendary, figure. His book on militarism, published in 1907, became one of the truly influential pacifist works during this war when, republished in a German underground edition, it helped radicalize German public opinion against the war. Cited in the U.S. press, quoted by French statesmen, published in England, idolized in Barbusse's pacifist novel, Liebknecht fired the imagination of all opponents of the war on both sides of the battle lines. His work also became a "landmark in the history of new revolutionism," a catalyst leading to the internal breakdown of the German empire.[1]

Yet Liebknecht's significance as a leader of the German and international Left has often been underestimated and cast in shadow by the ideological brilliance and intellectual originality of his friend and colleague, Rosa Luxemburg. Among those failing to give due credit to the historical significance of Liebknecht are liberal German historians whose views still dominate traditional German historiography. In addition to their excessive preoccupation with the

5

role of the state, with reigns, wars, ministries and individual statesmen, their elitist "mandarin view of history" has been said to overemphasize the role of ideas in German history to the neglect of social and economic conflict and change. Thus liberal history, exemplified by the work of such outstanding scholars as Hajo Holborn, has been called "history written by the middle class, for the middle class, about the middle class."[2] Similarly, the ideological and intellectual contributions of radical leaders like Liebknecht and Luxemburg are largely neglected by historians of German intellectual history who, however, devote painstaking care to the detailed recital of the most eccentric vagaries of right-wing movements.

By contrast, younger revisionist historians see World War I as the German ruling class' preventive reaction to potential revolution from the Left. Viewed from their vantage point, the Social Democratic Left of Liebknecht and Luxemburg, eventually culminating in the founding of the Communist Party of Germany (KPD), may be regarded as symbolic of the underlying social conflicts suppressed by the German empire.

But if the liberals are guilty of political and class bias, one must also view with some scepticism the writings of East German and Soviet hagiographers who, engaged in the Stalinist denigration of Luxemburg's democratic socialism, have elevated Liebknecht to a position almost superior to that of his ideologically far more original colleague.

INTRODUCTION

Karl Liebknecht was born in 1871, the son of Wilhelm Liebknecht, a founder of the Social Democratic Party of Germany. Young Liebknecht received the conventional education of the German intelligentsia and middle class. His law degree subsequently enabled him to defend his Social Democratic and radical comrades against government persecution. His anti-military propaganda was launched in the socialist youth movement, culminating in his trial and imprisonment for the views expressed in Militarism and Anti-Militarism, *published in 1907. In spite, or perhaps because, of this mark against him, the voters of Berlin subsequently elected him to the Prussian Diet in 1908, although hampered by the inequitable three-class system of voting which favored the conservative ruling groups. In 1912 the constituents of the working class district of Potsdam made him their representative in the imperial* Reichstag. *It is striking that a firebrand like Liebknecht spent a good part of his career as a member of the imperial Diet of William II's Germany.*

This fact may serve as a hint of the new social forces emerging from behind the rigidly conservative facade of the empire. Despite rapid industrialization Germany had failed to accommodate concomitant social and political changes; thus the state was able to impose its anachronistic political and social values on society, values which were accepted even by the reformist and revisionist Social Democratic Party.

By the first decade of the century the Social

7

Democrats, moribund and bureaucratized, had become a party of functionaries led by the oligarchy headed by Friedrich Ebert, who has been called "the Stalin of German Social Democracy."[3] *The sizeable and powerful trade union membership, preoccupied with immediate material rather than revolutionary goals, also served to push the party further to the right. Thus the Social Democrats made compromises on such major issues of socialist orthodoxy as nationalism and militarism to the extent of voting for army credits and accepting collaboration with the capitalist state in the* Reichstag.

Karl Liebknecht conducted a lifelong struggle against the bureaucratization of his party and from the beginning of his career he was at odds with the party's conservative leadership. A polarization of the party, leading to an eventual split, was accelerated at the outbreak of World War I when the Social Democrats accepted with relief the Burgfriede, *freedom from government persecution, offered to them in return for voting war credits out of "deference" for the imperialist and capitalist state they had come to fight. Meanwhile the more radical elements of the party formed the Independent Social Democratic Party (USPD), opposed to the continuation of the war. It soon appeared that the left wing of this party, led by Liebknecht's and Luxemburg's revolutionary Spartacus League, found even this accommodation far too conservative. Agreeing on ending the war, they disagreed with the Independents on such issues as the necessity of revolution and in December 1918 founded the Communist Party of Germany.*

Meanwhile the majority Social Democrats had come to feel that they had a stake in the regime and, seeing themselves as its heirs, accepted power after the collapse of the German empire at the end of a disastrous war. Identification with the goals of the old regime led to the Social Democrats' insistence on the importance of orderly transition following the collapse. Thus the first years of the Weimar regime under a coalition including the Social Democrats were not so much the beginning of a new era but an attempt to patch up the body of the ailing invalid: Wilhelmine Germany. Yet we must also trace the polarization of the party during the war to war-weariness, economic breakdown, as well as to the radicalizing effect of the Russian revolution.

As an ideologist Liebknecht was not the equal of Luxemburg, but he shared with her a number of common beliefs regarding party organization. Possibly as a result of their lifelong struggle against the dead weight of Social Democratic bureaucracy they tended to veer to the other extreme. They opposed party bureaucracy and centralization, believing that the masses had to develop their own road to spontaneous revolution sparked off by a general strike, seeing in the general strike a revolutionary weapon developed in the Russian revolution of 1905. Thus they rejected Lenin's concept that the minority party as a disciplined revolutionary elite should impose revolution on the masses from above. The tragic weakness of Spartacus, leading to the failure of the 1918-19 revolution and the assassination of Liebknecht and Luxemburg, also lent it moral strength, establishing a democratic, humanist strain in the Marxist movement that might have helped counter the totalitarian implications of the Leninist party machine.[5]

Liebknecht and Luxemburg, the two most prominent members of Spartacus, were almost alone among the Social Democratic leaders in their conviction that membership in the imperial Reichstag *must be used as a platform for class propaganda, a tactical weapon against imperialism, militarism, nationalism and capitalism. Unlike the majority Social Democratic leaders, Liebknecht used his position in the* Reichstag, *not to persuade his fellow-deputies, but to reach mass audiences outside the political arena.*[6]

Thus in 1913 Liebknecht used his Reichstag *position to launch an attack on the armaments industry, the Krupp cartel in particular, and asserted that its sales to France and other countries revealed the existence of an international armaments network directed against workers everywhere, demonstrating the supra-national solidarity of capitalism. Since he saw his role in the* Reichstag *as providing the opportunities to conduct an almost single-handed propaganda campaign against the war, it is not surprising that his motives and style were misunderstood even by his fellow-deputies in the*

Social Democratic delegation which expelled him during the war. He was often regarded as a "cantankerous crank," an irritating gadfly and rabble-rouser, and he was soon accused of treason.[7] *Karl Liebknecht's major contribution, his lifelong crusade, consisted of his recklessly courageous attack on militarism as a tool of the German empire and international capitalism.* Militarism and Anti-Militarism, *his best-known and most widely publicized work, was based on a speech Liebknecht presented to socialist youth groups at the 1906 congress of the Social Democratic Party. Throughout his life he devoted a great deal of attention to the socialist youth movement, aware of the paramount importance of winning youth for the antimilitarist cause before it could be reached by the regime's all-pervasive military propaganda, which offered youth a traditional and romantic cult of the fatherland, instilling the Prussian worship of army and state. One major obstacle to Liebknecht's youth crusade was the Social Democratic Party's insistence on curbing the autonomy and spontaneity of the youth movement, thus imposing the regimentation of the conservative party bureaucracy. It is significant that neither historians of the Social Democratic Party nor liberals give Liebknecht credit for his intensive work in the socialist youth movement.*[8]

In Militarism *and* Anti-Militarism *Liebknecht expressed his belief that militarism was closely identified with the goals of capitalist imperialism, to be fought on all fronts, but especially among youth, to make it perceive the insidious dangers of official militaristic indoctrination. Militarism, he insisted, served capitalism abroad through its naval and colonial policies, securing all profits from imperialist ventures for the ruling class. It also served the capitalist state at home, bolstering the internal order, thus preventing the economic strikes of the proletariat for higher wages and the political strikes for revolution. Liebknecht's formulation, less complex and sophisticated than Luxemburg's, expressed his acute awareness of the impact of the military on society. Extending beyond the military establishment itself, it saturated and swallowed up the entire society, wrapping its tentacles around every manifestation of German life.*

Liebknecht fulminated against the regime's maltreatment of soldiers, seething with a moral indignation characteristic of the ethical fervor of the German radical Left. His passionately hated target was the German military ethos with its "reserve officer myth," accepted by most Germans, including the majority Social Democrats who merely limited their criticism to the worst abuses of the army. They generally regarded the military as necessary for the defense of the German state.

In declaring that the military destroyed individualism, turned men into slaves or machines, Liebknecht asserted a belief in the autonomy and dignity of the individual, espousing the same humanist values

*of Western civilization represented by Marx's ago-
nized cry against the alienation of men exposed to
the harshness of industrial society, reducing joyous
and creative individuals into appendages of the
machine. Thus Liebknecht insisted that the sole
weapon against this militaristic dehumanization of
man required instilling in youth an abiding hatred of
the military. Luxemburg's own writings shared this
humanist emphasis which foreshadowed the later
thought of Georg Lukács, as well as the more recent
revisionist school of "socialist humanism" based both
on the discovery of the youthful writings of Marx,
and the more immediate response against the Stalinist
heritage.*

*Liebknecht made a similar appeal to the classical,
humanist values of Western civilization when he
attacked the brutalizing nature of German wartime
education in his* Reichstag *speech of 1916: "You
abhor the free mind because it will mean the twilight
of the gods of the ruling classes. Classical education
of today is only a parody on real classical education."
The essence of the classics, he stated, was "the spirit
of humanism, the spirit of independence, of clear
vision, of criticism of everything which is felt to be
harmful. This is the real freedom of the spirit."[9]*

The publication of Militarism and Anti-Militarism
*led to Liebknecht's trial and conviction to a term in
prison, of which he served eighteen months, for
attacking the German military. He used his trial, as he
later used his* Reichstag *platform, to reach a wide*

INTRODUCTION

segment of people with his anti-military propaganda. This Don Quixote of the German Left undoubtedly saw himself as destined to martyrdom, exalted by his symbolic mission in fighting for the revolution, rather than as an ideologist or party organizer.

Upon his release he continued the antimilitarist struggle in the Prussian Diet and the Reichstag, *although when war broke out he first followed party discipline by voting for war credits against his better judgment. By December 1914 he could no longer vote against his conscience and became the first Social Democrat to refuse to do so. Meanwhile he continued to agitate against the war and the resulting military oppression, developing the theme that "the main enemy is at home."[10] After a mass May Day demonstration in 1916 he was again arrested and imprisoned. In this speech he called for the war's end, declaring: "By a lie the German workingman was forced into the war, and by like lies they expect to induce him to go on with war!"[11] After release from prison in 1918 he threw himself into the flood tides of revolution brought about by war-weariness, economic hardship and military defeat. By then he had become a hero who even outshone Luxemburg in his popularity with the masses, as well as with the international Left.[12]*

No account of Liebknecht's career can explain the wide appeal of the man without attempting to portray his public and private personality which has attracted both unreasoning hatred and overwhelming

14

devotion. He had none of the bureaucratic greyness of the Social Democratic functionary. Impetuous and flamboyant, he was capable of demonstrating enormous warmth and tenderness privately, while maintaining a strident militancy in public.

He was a tender, loving, even sentimental husband and father. His letters to his wife and children, written first from the front and later from prison, are filled with concern, advice, encouragement and boundless affection. This was a different side of the man whom "privileged Germany" regarded as a dangerous troublemaker. He described his prison readings: the classics, including Homer, Schiller, Goethe, Shakespeare, Sophocles, and ranging through French and English literature. He urged his sons to follow his example to attain a rich future possible only through a deep and wide general education. In the tone reminiscent of any bourgeois parent he insisted that they must "study, study and study some more." [13]

Loving nature, he reflected on the coming of spring, and described his joy at hearing the song of the nightingale and the wild dove, at seeing the sky and branches of a tree through his prison bars. Rosa Luxemburg commented that beneath all the militancy Liebknecht had a "poetical nature." [14]

In his public role he was an impressive orator whom Wilhelm Pieck, later Communist leader of the German Democratic Republic, had called a "Volkstribun." [15] *And certainly many of his conservative colleagues in the* Reichstag, *both within and outside the party, saw him as a demagogue and even a madman. Rosa Luxemburg, whose sense of irony spared neither herself nor her friends, left this unforgettable and derisive word-portrait of his wartime behavior:*

> *You probably know the manner of his existence for many years: entirely wrapped up in parliament, meetings, commissions, discussions; in haste, in hurry, everlastingly jumping from the underground into the tram and from the tram into a car. Every pocket stuffed with notebooks, his arms full of the latest newspapers which he will never find the time to read, body and soul covered with street dust and yet always with a kind and cheerful smile on his face.*[16]

She admired his courage but deplored his hotheadedness, regarding him, especially during the critical days of the revolution, as unduly reckless and undisciplined, and attacking his tendency to "Putschism." During the last months of their lives, while already hunted by the government, she described his excitement in the revolution, clearly the highest point in his life, by commenting that "in spite of his exhaustion he was happy as a child."[17]

In January 1919 Luxemburg and Liebknecht reluctantly yielded to the inchoate yearning of the masses for an uprising, realizing that the lack of organization of the revolutionaries, including Spartacus with its anti-bureaucratic anarcho-syndicalist bias, doomed the action to certain failure. Thus they allied themselves with such groups as the Independent Social Democrats of Berlin, the revolutionary shop stewards and the People's Marines, groups that had already been active in revolutionary action. The utopian faith of Liebknecht and Luxemburg in the spontaneity of the masses, their belief, in contrast to Lenin's, that the masses must lead and the party follow, led them into revolution and certain death.

As they correctly foresaw, the revolution was suppressed by the coalition government of the new German republic, in which the majority Social Democrats played an important role; Liebknecht and Luxemburg were hunted down and murdered by the members of the Free Corps, organized by the Social Democratic War Minister Noske. Both Liebknecht and Luxemburg considered that it was their duty and an honor to sacrifice their lives for a socialist revolution regardless of its success.[18]

Marian A. Low
John Jay College — C.U.N.Y.

INTRODUCTION

NOTES

[1]*Carl E. Schorske*, German Social Democracy: 1905-1917 *(New York: John Wiley and Sons, 1955), p. 339.*

[2]*Geoffrey Barraclough, "Mandarins and Nazis: Part I," The New York Review of Books, November 16, 1972, p. 25.*

[3]*Schorske, p. 124.*

[4]*Ibid.*

[5]*Ibid., pp. 318, 323.*

[6]*J.P. Nettl, Rosa Luxemburg (2 vols.; London: Oxford University Press, 1966), I, 236; II, 619 ff.*

[7]*Karl W. Meyer, Karl Liebknecht: Man without a Country (Washington, D.C.: Public Affairs Press, 1957), p. 76; Nettl, p. 623.*

[8]*Schorske, pp. 97-102, 211. For a Social Democratic version of the history of the socialist youth movement in which Liebknecht is almost completely ignored see: Karl Korn:* Die Arbeiterjugendbewegung: Einführung in ihre Geschichte *(Berlin: Arbeiterjugendverlag, 1922, 1923). Recent histories of the German youth movement tend to overlook the socialist youth movement almost altogether. See Walter Z. Laqueur:* Young Germany: A History of the German Youth Movement *(New York: Basic Books, 1962).*

[9]*Karl Liebknecht: "The Future Belongs to the People" (New York: Macmillan, 1918), p. 108.*

[10]*Nettl, II, p. 615.*

[11]*Liebknecht, p. 134.*

[12]*Nettl, II, pp. 658-660.*

[13]*Liebknecht:* Briefe aus dem Felde, aus dem Untersuchungshaft und aus dem Zuchthaus *(Berlin-Wilmersdorf: Verlag die Aktion, 1922), p. 11.*

[14]*Nettl, II, p. 636.*

[15]*Institut fur Marxismus-Leninismus beim ZK der SED,* Karl Liebknechts Vermächtnis für die Deutsche Nation *(5 vols.; Berlin: Dietz Verlag, 1962-   ), I, p. 144.*

18

NOTES

[16] *Nettl, II, p. 636.*
[17] Ibid., *II, p. 760.*
[18] Ibid., *II, p. 781.*

MILITARISM AND ANTI-MILITARISM

With Special Regard to the
International Young Socialist
———— Movement ————

BY

DR. KARL LIEBKNECHT

Printed and Published by
SOCIALIST LABOUR PRESS,
50 Renfrew Street, Glasgow.

Dr Karl Liebknecht.

CONTENTS.

Part I.—MILITARISM.

PAGE

CHAP. I.—GENERAL REMARKS, ...   1
About the Essence and Meaning of Militarism—
Origin and Basis of Social Relations of Power—
A Few Items from the History of Militarism.

CHAP. II.—CAPITALIST MILITARISM, ...   11
Preliminary Remark—Militarism "Against the
Enemy Abroad," Navalism and Colonial Mili-
tarism. Possibilities of War and Disarmament—
Proletariat and War—Characteristics of Mili-
tarism "Against the Enemy at Home" and its
Task.   .   .   .

CHAP. III.—METHODS AND EFFECTS OF MILITARISM,   22
The Immediate Object — Militarist Pedagogy.
Education of the Soldier—Semi-official and Semi-
military Organization of the Civil Population—
Other Military Influences on the Civil Population
—Militarism as Machiavelianism and as a Political
Regulator.

CHAP. IV.—PARTICULARS OF SOME OF THE
CHIEF SINS OF MILITARISM,   ..   42
Ill-treatment of Soldiers, or Militarism as a Penitent
yet Incorrigible Sinner—Cost of Militarism, or
La Douloureuse—The Army as a Tool against the
Proletariat in the Economic Struggle. Preliminary
Remark—Soldiers as Competitors of Free Labourers
—Army and Blacklegging — Right of the Sword
and the Rifle in Strikes. Preliminary Remark—
Italy — Austria-Hungary — Belgium — France —
United States of America—Canada—Switzerland—
Norway—Germany—Military Societies and Strikes
—The Army as a Tool against the Proletariat in
the Political Struggle, or the Right of the Cannon
—Military Societies in the Political Struggle—
Militarism, a Menace to Peace—Difficulties of a
Proletarian Revolution.

Part II.—ANTI-MILITARISM.

PAGE

CHAP. I.—ANTI-MILITARISM OF THE OLD AND THE NEW INTERNATIONAL, ..   89

CHAP. II. — ANTI-MILITARISM ABROAD, WITH SPECIAL REGARD TO THE YOUNG SOCIALIST ORGANIZATIONS, ...   95
Belgium — France — Italy — Switzerland — Austria — Hungary — Holland — Sweden — Norway — Denmark — America — Spain — Finland—Russia—International Anti-militarist Organization.

CHAP. III.—THE DANGERS BESETTING ANTI-MILITARISM, ...   137

CHAP. IV.—ANTI-MILITARIST TACTICS, ...   142
(1) Tactics against Militarism Abroad—(2) Tactics against Militarism at Home—(3) Anarchist and Social-Democratic Anti-Militarism.

CHAP. V.—THE NEED FOR SPECIAL ANTI-MILITARIST PROPAGANDA, ..   161

CHAP. VI.—ANTI-MILITARISM IN GERMANY AND THE GERMAN SOCIAL-DEMO-CRACY, ...   165

CHAP. VII.—THE ANTI-MILITARIST TASKS OF THE GERMAN SOCIAL-DEMO-CRACY, ...   173

PREFACE TO THE ENGLISH EDITION.

SOON after Karl Liebknecht published his work, "Militarism and Anti-Militarism," it was confiscated by the German authorities, and the author was tried for high treason at Leipzig, Saxony, in October, 1907. The trial commenced on 9th October and lasted three days. Throughout the whole of the trial the court was crowded with Liebknecht's sympathizers.

The proceedings were begun by the presiding judge in his red robe (the fourteen judges who sat with him were also in red robes), who read the following preliminary indictment drawn up on 9th August, 1907 :

" By order of the Imperial state attorney, in accordance with paragraph 138 of the law concerning the judicial procedure of the Imperial courts, the main proceedings are opened before the united 2nd and 3rd criminal chambers of the Imperial court, against Dr. Karl Paul August Friedrich Liebknecht, lawyer, of Berlin, who is suspected of having set on foot a treasonable undertaking in the years 1906 and 1907 within the country : that of effecting a change in the constitution of the German Empire by violence, viz. : abolition of the standing army by means of the military strike, if needs be conjointly with the incitement of troops to take part in the revolution, by writing the work " Militarism and Anti-Militarism," and causing it to be printed and disseminated, in which he advocated the organization of special anti-militarist propaganda which was to extend throughout the whole Empire, and conjointly with it the setting up a Central Committee for conducting and controlling same, and making use of the Social-Democratic Young People's Organizations for the purpose of organically disintegrating and demoralizing the militarist spirit ; the necessary sequence of which would be—in the case of an unpopular war and in exceptional cases even to-day : such as in the case of a war between France and Germany or in the case of Germany's intervention in Russia—the military strike and the eventual incitement of troops to take part in the revolution ; that is to say, he not only pointed out the ways and means which appear to be destined and suited to further the aforesaid treasonable undertaking and to insure its success, but he also demanded the speedy application of these methods (crime against paragraph 86 of the criminal code in connection with par. 81, No. 2, par. 82 of the criminal code).

" The order for the confiscation of the aforesaid work remains in full force.   The accused is not to be subjected to preliminary confinement."

Throughout the proceedings Liebknecht bore himself in a manly way.   He took upon himself the full responsibility for what was contained in the work, but he fiercely contested all the insinuations made by the public prosecutor and the wrong ideas that he tried to read into his work.   He repeated several times that it was absurd to put him on his trial for treason, for nowhere in the book had he advocated illegal action, that his trial was purely a political affair and that his condemnation was a foregone conclusion.

The public prosecutor asked the court to pass a sentence of two years' imprisonment and the loss of civil rights for five years.   After deliberating for half-an-hour the court passed the following sentence :

" The accused is found guilty of having set on foot a treasonable undertaking and is condemned to incarceration in a fortress for eighteen months.   The costs of the prosecution are to be paid by the accused.

" All copies of the work ' Militarism and Anti-militarism ' which has been put under the ban, in the possession of the author, printer, publisher, wholesale booksellers and booksellers, as well as all publicly exposed copies of this work, or those offered for sale, as well as the plates and forms for their production, are to be destroyed."

Thousands of people, chiefly working men and working women, had ga hered in the lobbies and outside the court discussing the outcome of the trial. When Comrade Liebknecht appeared outside he was vociferously cheered by the crowd ; this proved the workers' appreciation of the stand he was taking against German militarism and against militarism in general.

Liebknecht states in his work that the semi-republican and republican countries (with the exception of Great Britain) have been the chief offenders as regards employing the armed forces of the state in bloody conflicts with the strikers. What Liebknecht contended in 1907 has been substantiated in a most striking manner not only as regards France, the United States of America and Australia, but also Great Britain. In the great Coal and Railway strikes of 1911 the British Government lent the whole force of the State to defeat the strikers,* and the workers' blood was spilt. The French Railway strike of 1910 has become a classical example. Briand challenged the workers to choose between allegiance to their class organization or to the capitalist state, and scored a signal victory. In Colorado, U.S.A., there was a feud between the Rockefeller interests and the strikers, which culminated in the bestial massacre of workers at Ludlaw camp. As the life interests of the bourgeoisie in the various countries became seriously threatened it never failed to show its ugly claws.

As regards " Militarism against the enemy abroad," Liebknecht, in lectures and in the Press, repeatedly called upon the German Social-Democracy to take up the question of militarism in a serious manner. In the present work he makes the following appeal : " And we keep asking : ' Is German Social-Democracy, the German Labour movement—the nucleus and the *elite* troop of the new International, as it likes to be called—being

---

* Mr. Asquith told the Railwaymen :—His Majesty's Government will place the whole civil and military forces of the Crown at the disposal of the Railway Companies.

either too prudent or over-confident is German Social-Democracy going to refrain from tackling this problem till, inadequately armed and straining to the utmost all its strength and its methods of fighting, it is faced by the fact of a world war or an intervention in Russia, which can to a certain extent be avoided and for which German Social-Democracy would also have to bear the responsibility ? ' ''

But his appeals fell upon deaf ears. Liebknecht's ideas were actively opposed by Bebel and other influential leaders of German Social-Democracy. This attitude was plainly manifested at the Stuttgart congress of 1907. Vaillant, on behalf of the French delegation, proposed definite methods of fighting militarism. Bebel, on the other hand, said that German Social-Democracy did not want to commit itself to a definite course of action, but that when the time for action came it would know how to act.

The present war has demonstrated that the policy of the German leaders was an ostrich-like policy : though scenting danger they stuck their heads in the sand, perhaps lulled into a false sense of security by the increasing Socialist vote in Germany. But this policy contains two palpably weak points :—(1) It is absurd to entertain the idea that the mass of the workers need not bother their heads about militarism and that when the times comes *the leaders will tell them what to do ;* (2) A political organization (unless it is backed up by an industrial organization of the workers) is not an instrument that can be used effectively because it is impossible to mobilize the voters for action at a critical moment. The Socialist movement (in its bulk) made straight for disaster with its eyes blindfolded and it was wrecked on the shoals of the present war. The proletariat should take to heart the lessons of the past and set to work to solve the urgent problems now confronting it as regards militarism.

Tackling militarism means tackling a hornet's nest. Bebel who gave evidence at Liebknecht's trial, said he was opposed to a special anti-militarist organization being started in Germany. Amongst other things he stated : " First I said to myself that the comrades who would carry on the agitation have not had such a good legal training as the accused (Liebknecht) and, therefore, they would soon come into collision with paragraph 112 of the Criminal Code, which is such an unpleasant contingency that we would rather not have our comrades face it. Finally, I have opposed the tactics of the accused because I know there are large influential sections in Germany which are waiting for a chance to make a decisive onslaught on Social-Democracy either by rendering the provisions of the Criminal Code more stringent or by passing a special law."

The German Social-Democrats refrained from making a serious onslaught upon militarism because they preferred not to run the risk of having their organization disrupted or their members brutally punished. But if we really believe in our ideal of international Socialism we must be willing to face risks. The Prussian Junker lays down his life that his caste may dominate, the German Socialist Patriot calmly faces the bullets of the enemy that Germany may live, and the French nationalist dies for his country ; the Russian Socialists have died in thousands in the Tsar's unhealthy prisons, in the gold-mines of Siberia and the benumbing cold of the Arctic zone. People are willing to suffer and die for the most varied ideals. If our proletarian ideal of international Socialism is worth anything we must be prepared to give our time, our health, even our life for its realization. Comrade Liebknecht has set us a splendid example. On 1st May, 1916, he threw down the gauntlet to the German Government at a public meeting, and he is now pining behind prison walls for his brave deed. The letters (dated 3rd and 8th May) he addressed to the Royal Court Martial in Berlin express in a nutshell the creed of an international Socialist. Liebknecht appeals to the international proletariat as follows :

" The present war is not a war for the defence of national integrity, nor for the liberation of downtrodden people, nor for the benefit of the masses. From the point of view of the proletariat it only signifies the greatest possible concentration and intensification of political oppression, of economic exploitation and of the wholesale military slaughter of the working class for the benefit of Capitalism and absolutism.

" To this the working class of all countries can give but one answer : A harder struggle, the international class struggle against the capitalist governments and the ruling classes of all countries for the abolition of oppression and exploitation, for the termination of the war by a peace in the Socialist spirit. In this class struggle is included the defence of everything that a Socialist— whose fatherland is the International—has to defend.

" The cry, ' Down with the war ! ' is meant to express that I thoroughly condemn and oppose the present war because of its historical essence, because of its general social causes and the particular form of its origin, because of its methods and its aims ; and the cry is also meant to express that it is the duty of every representative of proletarian interests to take part in the international class struggle for its termination."

ALEXANDER SIRNIS.

July, 1917.

PREFACE.

A FEW weeks ago the *Grenzbote* reported a conversation which took place between Bismarck and Dr. Otto Kaemmel in October, 1892. In this conversation the " Hero of the Century " himself threw off the mask of constitutionalism with the cynicism peculiar to him. Amongst other things, Bismarck said :

" He who in Rome put himself outside the pale of the law was banished (*aqua et igni interdictus*) ; in the Middle Ages he was said to be outlawed. Social-Democracy should be similarly treated and deprived of its political rights. I would have gone to this length. *The Social-Democratic question is a mili'ary question.* At present Social-Democracy is not taken seriously enough ; it strives—and successfully—to win over the non-commissioned officers. In Hamburg a large portion of the troops already consists of Social-Democrats, for the inhabitants have the right to join the local battalions only. Suppose these troops should one day refuse to fire on their fathers and brothers at the Emperor's order ? Should we have to mobilize the Hanover and Mecklenburg regiments against Hamburg ? We should, in that case, have something like the Paris Commune. The Emperor took fright. He told me that he did not wish to be called the " *Kartaetschenprinz* " (Shrapnel prince) some day, like his grandfather, and did not wish to " *wade up to his ankles in blood* " at the very *beginning* of his reign. I answered him at the time : " *Your Majesty will have to wade much deeper* if you draw back now."

" *The Social-Democratic question is a military question.*" This puts the whole problem in a nutshell. This expresses more and goes much deeper than von Massow's cry of distress : " Our only hope lies in the bayonets and cannons of our soldiers."* " *The Social-Democratic question is a military question.*" This is now the keynote of all tunes sung by the firebrands. If there was anyone whose eyes had not yet been opened by the earlier indiscretions of Bismarck and Puttkamer, by the speech to the Alexandrians,† the *Hamburger Nachrichten* and the thoroughbred Junker von Oldenburg-Januschau, this would now be accomplished by the Hohenlohe-Delbrück revelations confirmed about the end of the year by the county court judge Kulemann, and by the above heartless words of Bismarck.

" *The Social-Democratic question—to the extent that it is a political question—is in the last resort a military question.*" This should be a constant warning to the Social-Democracy and a *tactical principle of first importance.*

The enemy at home (Social-Democracy) is " more dangerous than the enemy abroad, because it poisons the soul of our people and wrenches the weapon from our hands before we have raised it." Thus the *Kreuzzeitung*, of 21st January, 1907, announced that class interests come before national interests in an electoral fight which was carried on " under the waving flag of Nationalism." And over this electoral fight hung the ever-increasing menace to the electoral rights and the right of Trade Union organization, the menace of " Bonaparte's Sword " which, in his letter of New Year's eve Prince Buelow flourished round the heads of the German Social-Democrats in order to intimidate them. This electoral fight was carried on under the banner of the class struggle at its fiercest.‡ Only one who is

---

* *Vide Das Deutsche Wochenblatt Arendts*, middle November, 1896. *Sozialdemokratische Parteikorrespondenz*, II. year, No. 4.

† Speech delivered by the Kaiser to the recruits of the Alexander regiment calling upon them to shoot at their fathers and mothers.—*Trans.*

‡ On the evening of 5th February, 1907, when the second ballots were taken, troops of the Berlin garrison were provided with live cartridges and held ready to march. It is known that on 25th June, 1903, when the second ballots were last taken, in Spandau pioneers appeared in the Schoenwaller Stra se to " bring to their senses " the workers excited by the result of the elections.

blind and deaf could deny that these and many other signs pointed to a storm, even to a hurricane.

Thus the problem of fighting " militarism at home " has become of the greatest importance.

The Carnival elections of 1907 were also fought on the nationalist question, on the colonial question, on Chauvinism and Imperialism. And they showed, in spite of all this, how miserably small was the power of resistance of the German people against the pseudo-patriotic traps laid by these despicable business patriots. They taught us what bombastic demagogy can be employed by the Government, the ruling classes, and the whole howling pack of " patriots " when the " things they hold most holy " are concerned. These elections furnished the proletariat with the necessary enlighten-ment ; they caused it to bethink itself and taught it the social and political relation of forces. They educated it and freed it from the unfortunate " habit of victory." These elections rendered the proletarian movement more profound by exerting a desirable pressure on it, and enabled one to understand the psychology of the masses in regard to national acts. Certainly the causes of our so-called setback (which, in reality, was no setback, and by which the victors were more taken aback than the vanquished) were manifold. But there is no doubt that just those sections of the proletariat which have been contaminated and influenced by militarism formed an especially solid obstacle which prevents the spreading of Social-Democracy. They were, for instance, state workers and lower-grade officials who are at the mercy of governmental terrorism.

This, too, forces the question of anti-militarism and the question of the young people's movement and of their education to the fore ; and the German Labour movement will henceforth certainly pay more attention to these points.

The following brochure is the enlargement of a paper read by the author on 28th November, 1906, at the

Mannheim Conference of the German Young Socialist organizations. It does not pretend to offer anything essentially new ; it only presumes to be a compilation of material already known. Nor does it pretend to exhaust the subject. The author has endeavoured, as far as possible, to collect the disconnected material scattered in papers and magazines all over the world. And thanks especially to our Belgian comrade De Man it has been possible to give a short account of the anti-militarist and Young Socialist movement in the most important countries.

If mistakes have crept in here and there they should be excused on account of the difficulty of mastering the material and, frequently, by reason of the unreliability of the sources of information.

In the realm of militarism many things change quickly at the present time. What, for instance, is said further on in regard to French and English military reforms will very soon be rendered out-of-date by events.

This is still more true of anti-militarism and the proletarian Young Socialist movement, these latest manifestations of the proletarian struggle for freedom. They develop quickly everywhere, and one is glad to see them make headway in spite of setbacks now and then. Since this brochure was set up in type I have learned that the Finnish Young Socialist societies held their first congress in Tammersfors, on 9th and 10th December, 1906, where a union of youthful workers was founded. Apart from educating the class-consciousness of youthful workers, the special object of this union is to fight militarism in all its aspects.

People will be inclined to complain that the theoretical principles of our work are too briefly stated and their historical depth not sufficiently probed. In reply to this I must point out that the political aim of this brochure is to propagate anti-militarist thought.

Some people again will be dissatisfied with the piling up of countless details, often seemingly unimportant, especially in regard to the history of the Young Socialist movement and anti-militarism. This dissatisfaction may be justified. The author started from the assumption that only through details is one enabled to see clearly the upward and downward movement in the development of the organization, the moulding and changing of the tactical principles and the manner in which their application has been arrived at. One has to take into account that it is just detail that presents the chief difficulty in anti-militarist agitation and organization.

Dr. Karl Liebknecht.

Berlin, 11*th February*, 1907.

PUBLISHERS' NOTE.

The Socialist Labour Press feels that no apology or explanation is needed to introduce "Militarism and Anti-Militarism" to the English-speaking working-class, nor is there any need to introduce the author, Karl Liebknecht, whose brave fight against militarism has stirred and encouraged anti-militarist Socialists all over the world. We would, however, call attention to the fact that the publication of this work is an equal challenge to British militarism as it is to German militarism.

Karl Liebknecht does not attack German militarism because it is German, but because it is the duty of the international anti-militarist to attack the jingoes of his own nationality. Liebknecht pointed this out clearly in the statement he made to the Royal Court Martial at Berlin, May 8th, 1916. He said it was the duty of the internationalist to attack the enemy nearest home, viz., those of his own country. In support of this contention, he said :

> " If the German Socialists, for instance, were to combat the English Government and the English Socialists the German Government, it would be a farce or something worse. He who does not attack the enemy, Imperialism, represented by those who stand opposed to him face to face, but attacks those from whom he is far away and who are not within his shooting range, and that even with the help and approbation of his own Government (*i.e.*, those representatives of Imperialism who alone are directly opposed to him) is no Socialist, but a miserable hack of the ruling class. Such a policy is not class war, but its opposite—inciting to war."

Liebknecht's attitude was the correct one for him to take up : and it is one that the S.L.P. in this country has maintained right throughout the war. We have resolutely fought British junkerdom, and to-day, as before, we call upon the working-class to range itself under our banner and carry on the fight against militarism and capitalism until the same are overthrown and the world-wide international Socialist Republic is raised in place of the present time world-wide hell of militarism and capitalism.

The Cause of the working-class all over the world is one ; and the enemy of the working-class is one—the capitalist class. Unite ! Comrades ! and carry on the war against war—and against capitalism.

S. L. PRESS.

July, 1917.

PART I.

MILITARISM.

CHAPTER I.

GENERAL REMARKS.

ABOUT THE ESSENCE AND MEANING OF MILITARISM.

MILITARISM—one of the most oft-repeated war-cries of our time—denotes a phenomenon at once intricate, complex, many-sided, and at the same time most interesting and significant by reason of its origin and nature, its methods and effects. It is a phenomenon deeply rooted in the life of class-organized societies, yet it can assume within similar social systems the most varied forms, according to the special natural, political, social, and economic conditions of individual states and territories.

Militarism is one of the most important and most vital manifestations of the life of most social systems, because it expresses in the strongest, most concentrated and exclusive form the national, cultural, and class instinct of self-preservation.

A history of militarism written in its full meaning reveals the inner nature of the story of human evolution and its driving power. A dissection of capitalist militarism means the laying bare of the most secret and the finest rootlets of capitalism. The history of militarism is at the same time a history of the political, social, economic and, in general, the cultural relations of tension between states and nations, as well as a

B   I

history of the class struggles within individual state and national units.

It is plain that there can be no question here of even an attempt at such a history. But we will indicate a few general points.

ORIGIN AND BASIS OF SOCIAL RELATIONS OF POWER.

The deciding factor in every social relation of power is, in the last resort, the superiority of *physical force,** which, as a social phenomenon, does not appear in the form of the greater physical strength of some individuals. Moreover, on an average, one human being equals another, and a purely numerical proportion decides who is in the majority. This proportion of numbers does not simply correspond to the numerical proportion of those groups of persons whose interests are contradictory, but is determined chiefly by the extensive and intensive degree of the class consciousness, the intellectual and moral development of an individual class, since not everyone knows his real interests, especially his fundamental interests ; and, above all, not everyone recognises or acknowledges the interests of his class as his own individual interests. This intellectual and moral stage is determined by the economic position of individual groups of interests (classes), whilst the social and political position represents more a consequence (though one that reacts strongly) and an expression of the relation of power.

Economic superiority also helps *directly* to displace and to confuse the numerical proportion, because economic pressure not only influences the height of the intellectual and moral stage and, thereby, the recognition of class interests, but also produces a tendency to act

---

* And, of course, of the intellectual force which is a regulator inseparable from physical force to the extent that it effects the best possible use of the physical force and the subjugation of the physical force of men ; in fact, doing it through the medium of the physical force at its disposal thus acquired. As a rule it depends chiefly upon the economic position of the groups of interests to what extent the subjugation of the physical force exists as a social phenomenon, *i.e.*, aids in determining the social relation of power when it occurs on a large scale and with regularity in the dealings between individual groups of interests. Some of the more important aspects of this manifestation will be discussed later.

in conformity with more or less well understood class
principles. That the political machinery of the governing
class lends it increased power to " correct " the numerical
proportion in favour of the ruling group of interests is
taught us by all the well-known institutions such as :
the police, justice, schools, and the Church which must
also be included here. These institutions are set up
through the political machinery and employed in an administrative capacity. The first two work chiefly by
threats, intimidation and violence : the school chiefly by
blocking up all those channels by which class-consciousness might reach the brain and the heart : the Church
most effectively by blinding the people to present evils
and awakening their desire for the joys of a future life,
and by terrifying them with threats of the torture
chamber in hell.

But even the numerical proportion thus acquired
does not decide absolutely the relation of power. A
weapon in the hands of an armed man increases his
physical strength many times. It depends upon the
development of the technique of arms (including outer
fortification and strategy whose form is chiefly a
consequence of the technique of arms) how many times
this power is multiplied. The intellectual and economic
superiority of one group of interests over another is
turned into a downright physical superiority through
the possession of armaments, or of better armaments,
on the part of the superior class. Thus the possibility
is created of a class-conscious minority completely
dominating a class-conscious majority. Even when
the division into classes is determined by the
economic position, the political relation of power
of the classes is regulated by the economic position
of individuals only in the first place ; it is regulated
in the second place through the countless intellectual,
moral, and physical means at the disposal of the
economically dominant class. The concentration of
all this power exerts no influence on the constitution
of the classes, for this constitution is created by a
situation which does not depend upon it. This situation

forces certain classes (which themselves may constitute a majority), as if in accordance with nature's bidding, into economic dependence on other classes which may form a small minority. The former remain in this state of dependence without the class struggle or any political means of power being able to bring about a change.* *So that the class struggle can only be a struggle to further class-consciousness which embraces the readiness for sacrifice and for revolutionary deeds in the interest of one's class—a struggle to capture those means of power which are of importance either in the creation or suppression of class-consciousness, as well as of those physical and intellectual means of power whose possession means the multiplication of physical force.*

From all this one may grasp what an important *role* is played by the technique of arms in social struggles. It depends upon this technique whether a minority, when there is no longer an economic necessity, still remains in a position to dominate, at least for a certain time, a majority *against its will* by military action which is " political action of the most concentrated type." Apart from the division of the classes the development of the relations of power is in reality everywhere closely bound up with the development of the technique of arms. As long as everyone—even he who is in the worst possible economic position—can produce arms which are essentially equally good under equally difficult conditions the majority principle and democracy will be the regular political form of society. As long as the above proposition holds good this should also be the case when an economic division into classes has taken place. The natural process of development is that the division into classes (the consequence of economic and technical development) runs parallel with the improvement of the technique of arms, including the art of fortification and strategy. Thereby the production of arms becomes more and more a specialized profession.

---

* " In the social production of their life men enter certain definite necessary relations which do not depend upon their will, relations of production which correspond to a definite stage in the evolution of their material forces of production."—MARX.

And further, as class domination as a rule corresponds to the economic superiority of one class over another, and as the improvement of the technique of arms continually renders the production of arms* more difficult and more expensive, such production of arms gradually becomes the monopoly of the economically ruling class, whereby the physical basis of democracy is done away with. Then the point is : he who is in possession is in the right. It may happen that the class which was once in possession of the political means of power, is able to retain its *political* domination, at least for a time, even after it has lost its economic superiority.

After what has been said above it is unnecessary to dwell here on the point that not only the form and the character of the political relations of power are determined by the technique of arms, but also the form and the character of the class struggles of the period.

It is not sufficient that all citizens are equally armed and in charge of their arms to permanently safeguard the domination of democracy. Merely an equal distribution of arms, as events in Switzerland have shown us, does not obviate the danger that this distribution may be done away with by a majority which is about to become a minority or even by a minority which is better organized for striking a blow. The whole population can only be armed equally and permanently when the production of arms is in the hands of the people.

The *role* of democratizing which the technique of arms can play has been clearly depicted by Bulwer in the remarkable Utopia, " The Coming Race," which is one of his less known works. In this book Bulwer presupposes such a high development of the technique that every citizen can at any moment achieve the most disastrous results by means of a small stick, easily

* Besides munitions and weapons of all kinds including the system of lighting, the fortresses and men-of-war to the arms proper belong, for example, the military system of communications (horses, waggons, bicycles, building of roads and bridges, ships on inland waters, railways, automobiles, telegraphs, wireless telegraphy, telephone, etc.). Nor should we forget the telescope, airships, photography, and war dogs.

procurable and loaded with a mysterious force resembling electricity. And, indeed, we can reckon with the possibility that the easy domination by man over the most powerful forces of nature—even if it be in the remote future—will reach a stage which will render the application of the technique of slaughter impossible, for it would mean the annihilation of the human race. Technical progress will bring it about that the making of arms, instead of being exploited by the plutocracy to a certain extent, will again to a certain extent become the possession of men on a wide basis of democracy.

A FEW ITEMS FROM THE HISTORY OF MILITARISM.

In the lower cultures which know no division into classes the weapon as a rule serves, not only as a means of defence, but at the same time as a working tool. The weapons and tools are of such a primitive character that anyone can easily procure them at any time (stones and sticks, spears with stone arrow heads, bows, etc.). As no division of labour worthy of note yet exists, apart from the most primitive of all divisions of labour (that between man and wife), and as all the members of the community, at any rate those of one sex, either male or female, fulfil about equal social functions, and as there are as yet no economic or political relations of power, the weapon cannot be used inside the community to support such relations of power. It could not be used as such a support even should relations of power exist. Alongside of a primitive technique of arms only democratic relations of power are possible.

If under this lower culture the weapon is used inside the community, at the most to settle individual conflicts, the situation is changed when a division into classes and a greater improvement in the technique of arms make their appearance. The primitive communism of the lower agricultural peoples with their constitution under which women dominated knows no social and, therefore, no political relations of class domination under normal circumstances. Generally militarism does not make its

appearance at all ; external complications compel them
to be ready for war and even produce temporary military
despotisms which, among the Nomadic peoples, is of
frequent occurrence, owing to the division into classes
which has, as a rule, preceded.

Let us recall the organization of the Greek and Roman
armies in which, corresponding to the division of the
classes, there existed a purely military hierarchy,
divided according to the class position of the individual ;
upon his class position depended the quality of the
armament.   Further, let us recall the feudal armies of
knights with their troops of squires mostly on foot who
were always much more badly armed and who, according
to Patrice Laroque, played more the part of assistants
to the combatants than that of active participants in
the conflict.   That at that time the arming of the lower
classes was tolerated at all and even aided is explained,
not so much by the fact that the state could offer little
security to the individual, thus making it necessary that
everyone should be armed, as by the necessity of the
nation or the state being armed in the case of a possible
attack upon or defence against the external enemy.
The differentiation in the armament of individual
classes of society always made it possible that the
technique of arms might be employed in maintaining or
setting up the relation of power.   The slave wars of
Rome throw remarkable light upon this aspect of the
question.

A significant light is thrown on the question by the
German Peasant War and the Wars of the German
Towns.   The direct reasons why the outcome of the
German Peasant War was unfavourable were the
military-technical superiority of the feudal armies of
the Church, in the first instance.   The Wars of the
Towns in the 14th century against these very armies
were successful, not only because at that period the
technique of firearms was exceptionally backward
(the reverse of what it was during the Peasant War of
1525), but, above all, in consequence of the great economic
power of the towns which, as locally circumscribed

centres of social interests brought together within narrow confines, the representatives of these interests, and that without any considerable admixture of conflicting interests.

Further, through the art of building the towns from the first, occupied a tactical position of the same importance as that of the feudal lords, the Church and the Emperor in their burgs and fortresses—this also presents a military-technical element (fortification).   Lastly, the production of arms was in the hands of the towns, and as their citizens were altogether superior as regards technical preparedness they vanquished the army of the knights.*

One must not lose sight of the important part played by the various classes of society either living together in the same locality or scattered amongst other classes, as an examination of the Peasant and the Town Wars in particular shows us.   When the class division coincides with the division in regard to locality the class struggle is rendered easier.   This circumstance not only helps to develop the class-consciousness, but also, from the technical point of view, aids the linking together of the class mates into a military organization and also aids the production and supply of arms.   This favourable grouping of the classes in regard to locality has stood all bourgeois revolutions† in good stead ; in the proletarian revolution it is almost entirely absent.‡

Also in the hired armies still existing in our day, just as in the case of armament, we find economic power turned into physical power according to the Mephistophelian maxim : " If I can pay for six stallions am I not entitled to their strength ? I drive away and am

---

* Also the development of Italy in the 15th century presents here the greatest interest, tempting one to investigate the question more fully. It confirms our fundamental conception throughout.

† Also in the Russian Revolution in its early stage. Especially characteristic amongst the numerous other proofs is the armed uprising in Moscow in December, 1905. The remarkable tenacity displayed is explained by the bulk of the town population co-operating with the not very numerous revolutionaries in the firing line. The tactics of town guerilla warfare, so brilliantly evolved in Moscow, will become epoch-making.

‡ Working together in factories, etc., and living together in working-class quarters, etc., must, nevertheless, be taken into consideration.

a proper man just as if I had twenty-four legs ! " ; and according to a further maxim : *divide et impera !* (" Divide and rule ! "). Both these maxims are applied in the so-called *élite* troops. On the other hand, the Italian *condottieri* show in a striking way—as the Praetorians once did—what political power is placed in the hands of those who possess weapons, military training and the art of strategy. The hired soldier reached out boldly after kings' crowns, played ball with them and became the natural heir to the supreme power in the state.* It is a phenomenon which we see repeated down to our day in times of excitement and war when the military power ready to strike rests in the hands of individuals : Napoleon and his generals, also Boulanger.

The history of the German Wars of Liberation teaches important lessons about the influence of the external political situation on the form of the military organization and of militarism in general. In the Coalition wars of 1806 against the French Revolution the feudal standing army of Frederick the Great was demolished by the citizen army of France. As the wars had ended so disastrously for them the helpless German governments were faced by the alternative : either to be constantly at the mercy of the Corsican conqueror or to defeat him with his own weapons—with a citizen army under a system of universal service. Their own desire to survive and the spontaneous impulse on the part of the people compelled them to choose the latter course. Then began the great period of the democratization of Germany and especially of Prussia, brought on by pressure from without which lessened for a time the political, social and economic tension at home. Money and enthusiastic fighters for freedom were wanted. The value of man increased. His social quality as a producer of values and a prospective payer of taxes and his natural physical quality as the embodiment of physical force and intelligence, of the capacity to become enthusiastic, acquired a decisive meaning and raised his rate of exchange, as is always the case in times

---

* *Vide* Burckhardt I., p. 22, etc.

of general danger. On the other hand, the influence of class differentiation went down. The " Prussian people" had, to put it in the jargon of military weeklies, " learnt to forget all their quarrels during long years of foreign rule." As often is the case, the financial and the military question played a revolutionizing *role*. Some economic, social and political obstacles were removed. Industry and commerce which were financially of prime importance were fostered as much as the petty bureaucratic spirit of Prussia-Germany would permit it. Even political liberties were introduced or, at least, promised. The people rose, the storm began to rage, the Scharnhorst-Gneisenau army under the system of universal service drove the " hereditary foe " back over the Rhine during the great Wars of Liberation. They set up a contemptible model to him who had convulsed the world and had undermined the France of the Great Revolution, although it was not even the kind of democratic organization that Scharnhorst and Gneisenau had wished to create. After the nigger (the German people) had done his duty he received suitable thanks from the House of Hapsburg. The Karlsruhe resolutions followed the Battle of the Nations at Leipsic, and one of the most important acts of the futile Metternich regime of perfidious and accursed memory was (after the pressure from without had been removed and all the reactionary devils at home had been let loose again) the abolition of the democratic army of the Wars of Liberation. The territories of Germany which stood on a high level of culture might have been ripe for such an army, but the dead weight of the East Elbean-Borussian lack of culture abruptly crushed the democratic army and nearly all the glories of the great rising of the people.

A superficial review of the development of the military organization finally shows one how closely dependent is the constitution and the size of the army not only on the social division, but in a still higher degree on the technique of arms. The revolutionizing action which, for instance, the discovery of firearms exerted in this direction is one of the most striking facts in the history of war.

Chapter II.

CAPITALIST MILITARISM.

Preliminary Remark.

THERE is nothing specifically capitalistic about militarism. Moreover, it is proper and essential to all systems of class society of which the capitalist system is the last. Capitalism, like any other system of class society, develops its own special variety of militarism* ; for militarism, by its very essence, is a means to an end, or to several ends, which vary in accordance with the kind of social system, and which can be attained in different ways in accordance with this variance. This is brought to light not only by the military organization, but also by the other attributes of militarism which manifest themselves when militarism carries out its tasks.

An army based on universal military service corresponds best to the capitalist stage of development. Although it is an army composed of the people, it is not a people's army but an army against the people, or is being shaped more and more with this end in view.

It appears either as a standing army or as militia. The standing army which is not a special feature of capitalism alone† appears as its most developed and even as its normal form. This will be shown later.

---

* Bernstein is wrong when he says in the *Vie Socialiste*, of 5th June, 1905, that the present-day militarist institutions are only a legacy inherited from the more or less feudal monarchy.

† *Vide* Russia, where special circumstances which did not grow out of the internal conditions helped to bring about this result. The hired armies, for instance, are standing armies on a basis different from that of universal military service. The Italian towns of the 15th century had a militia.—(BURCKHARDT, l.c., p. 327.)

MILITARISM " AGAINST THE ENEMY ABROAD," NAVALISM
    AND COLONIAL MILITARISM. POSSIBILITIES OF
    WAR AND DISARMAMENT.

The army of the capitalistic order of society as well
as that of other systems of class society serves a double
purpose.
It is first of all a national institution destined to
attack a foreign country or to be protection against
danger from without. In short, the army is destined
for use in international complications or, to use a military
expression, " against the external enemy."
The latest developments by no means do away with
this function of the army. For capitalism war is indeed,
to use the words of Moltke, " a link in God's world
order."* To be sure, in Europe itself there is the
tendency to do away with certain causes of war. It
becomes less and less probable that a war might break
out in Europe in spite of Alsace-Lorraine and the
anxiety caused by the French trinity : Clemenceau,
Pichon and Picquart, in spite of the Eastern question,
in spite of Pan-Islamism, and in spite of the revolution
now taking place in Russia. On the other hand, highly
dangerous sources of friction have arisen in consequence
of the commercial and political aims of expansion†
which are being pursued by the so-called civilized states.
These sources of friction have been handed down to us
by the Eastern question and by Pan-Islamism in the
first instance and have arisen in consequence of the
world policy, especially of colonial policy, which—as
Buelow himself acknowledged without reserve in the

---

* In the well-known letter to Bluntschli (December, 1880) he says : " Eternal
peace is a dream and not even a pleasant one, and war is a link in God's world
order. War brings to the surface the noblest virtues of man, namely : courage
and renunciation, faithfulness to one's duty, and readiness for sacrifice at the risk
of one's life. Without war the world would stagnate in materialism." A few
months previously Moltke had written as follows : " Each war is a national
catastrophe " (Complete Works, V, pp. 193 and 200), and in 1841 he had written
in an article in the *Augsburger Allgemeine Zeitung :* " We openly endorse the
idea of a general European peace, so much derided."
    † According to Huebler's tables the total value of the world's export trade
has risen from 75,224 millions (£3,761,200,000) in 1891 to 109,000 millions
(£5,450,000,000) in 1905.

German Reichstag on 14th November, 1906*,—bears in its womb† countless possibilities of conflict and which, at the same time, pushed more and more strenuously to the fore two other kinds of militarism : marinism and colonial militarism. We Germans can tell a thing or two about this development !

Marinism, or naval militarism, is the twin brother of militarism on land and has all the repulsive and malignant traits of the latter. At the present time it is not only the consequence but also the cause of international dangers, of the danger of a world war in a still higher degree than militarism.

When pious people and deceivers want to make us believe, for instance, that the tension between Germany and England‡ is merely due to misunderstandings, incitement by malicious newspaper writers, and to the boastful speeches of the bad musicians in the concert of diplomacy, we know better. We know that this tension is a necessary consequence of the ever-growing economic rivalry between England and Germany on the world market, *i.e.*, a direct consequence of unbridled capitalist development and of international competition. The Spanish-American war over Cuba, the Abyssinian war of Italy, the Transvaal war of England, the Sino-Japanese war, the adventure of the Great Powers in China, the Russo-Japanese war, even though their special causes and conditions are manifold, yet they all possess one great common feature, that of wars of expansion. If we recall the Anglo-Russian tension in Thibet, Persia and Afghanistan, the Japanese-American disagreement in the winter of 1906, and, finally, the Morocco conflict of glorious memory with its Franco-Spanish co-operation of December, 1906,§ we recognise

---

* " What to-day renders our position complicated and difficult are our oversea aims and interests."

† Moltke's views on this subject were very quixotic. According to him cabinet wars are a thing of the past but, on the other hand, he looks upon party leaders as dangerous and criminal provokers of war. The party leaders and the stock exchange ! Certainly now and then he has clear insight.—(Complete Works 3, 1 p. 1, etc., 126, 135, 138.)

‡ Which is characterized by the fantastic abortion of English lingoism, entitled " The Invasion of 1910."

§ France, in the year 1906, as a result of the Morocco dispute, spent more than 100 millions (£5,000,000) to secure its Eastern frontier.

that the capitalist policy of expansion and colonial policy have placed countless mines under the edifice of world peace. The fuses are held by most varied hands, and the mines may easily and unexpectedly explode.* Certainly a time may come when the partition of the world has progressed so far that one may expect the trustification of all possible colonial possessions by the states owning colonies, *i.e.*, the elimination of colonial competition between states as has been achieved in regard to private competition between capitalists in the cartels and trusts within certain limits. But we have to wait long for that, and it may be postponed to the remote future by the economic and national awakening of China alone.

So that all the alleged *plans of disarmament* for the time being appear merely as tomfoolery, empty talk, and attempts to hoodwink. They bear the stamp of the Tsar as the chief author of the Hague comedy.

Quite recently the soap bubble of the alleged disarmament by England has burst in a ludicrous way; the war minister Haldane, the alleged promoter of such intentions, has bluntly expressed his opposition to a reduction of the active forces and has been exposed and proven to be a militarist firebrand.† At the same time as the Anglo-French military convention rises above the horizon and at the same hour as the second Peace Conference is being prepared Sweden increases its navy; in America‡ and Japan the war budget is on the upgrade; in France the Clemenceau ministry emphasises the necessity for a strong army and navy by demanding

---

* *Vide* the debates of the budget commission at the beginning of December, 1906, about the alleged plan of Semler, the deputy representing the shipping interests of Hamburg, to capture Fernando Po by Jameson's method. The plan was never fully explained.

† It matters not that for the time being he is still opposed to universal military service which *The Kreuzzeitung* of 29th November, 1906, regrets, on the ground that " universal military service would educate the English people to a fuller understanding of the seriousness of war " ! In Germany, indeed, according to the wish of the knights of t e *Kreuzzeitung*, the only purpose of universal military service is to force sacrifices in life and property on the people, while the decision as to war and peace rests in the hands of those who feel least the seriousness of war. They even know how to appreciate democracy when they see it in *foreign* countries.

‡ *Vide* . . . Roosevelt's message of 4th December, 1906.

208 millions* (£10,400,000) more. At the same time the *Hamburger Nachrichten* states that faith in military armaments as the only salvation is the quintessence of the state of mind of the ruling classes of Germany, and the German people are favoured by the Government with further demands for increased war expenditure† after which even our Liberals eagerly reach out.‡ By this we can measure the *naiveté* displayed by the French senator d'Estournelles de Constant, a member of the Hague court of arbitration, in his latest article on the limitation of armaments.§ In fact, this political dreamer does not even need one swallow to make the summer of disarmament ; a sparrow is enough for him. Quite refreshing, as opposed to this, is the frank brutality with which the Great Powers participating in the conference let Stead's proposals drop and even fought against the disarmament question being put on the agenda of the second Conference.

The third offshoot of Capitalism in the military realm, *colonial militarism*, deserves a few words. The colonial army, that is to say, the standing colonial troops, not the colonial militia‖ presumably projected for German South-West Africa, nor still less the totally different militia of the almost autonomous English colonies, play for England an extremely important *role ;* its importance increases also for the other civilized states. In the case of England the colonial army, apart from fulfilling the task of oppressing the colonial " enemy

---

* Justified mainly by the Morocco conflict.

† Twenty-four and three-quarter millions (£1,250,000) for the navy, 51 millions (£2,500,000) for the army, seven millions (£350,000) interest, together an increase of about 83 millions (£4,150,000) as against the Budget of 1906-7 ! Further prospects of unlimited naval armaments are indicated by an obviously inspired article in the *Reichsboten*, of 21st December, 1906. In addition there is the enormous colonial war expenditure (China expedition, 454 millions (£22,700,000), South-West African rising up to the present 490 millions (£24,500,000), East African rising two millions (£100,000), etc.). The demand to ratify the expenditure has now (on 13th December, 1906) caused a conflict and the dissolution of the Reichstag.

‡ *Vide*, for instance, the *Berliner Tageblatt*, of 27th October, 1906. Especially the dubious bill introduced by Ablass on 13th December, 1906, and the Liberal electoral war-cry of 25th January, 1907.

§ *La Revue*, 1st October, 1906. The " results actually achieved " by the disarmament movement, referred to by the editor of the *Revue*, remain his own profound secret.

‖ Dernburg in the Reichstag sitting of 29th November, 1906.

at home " or keeping him in check (viz., the natives of
the colonies), is a force against the external colonial
enemy, for instance, Russia.   In the other states which
own colonies, especially America and Germany*, the
almost exclusive and primary task of the colonial army,
under the designation of a " defensive detachment " or
the " foreign legion,"† is to turn the unlucky natives
into serfs and to drive them into capitalist slavery.
When they wish to defend their fatherland against the
foreign conquerors and bloodsuckers, it is the duty of
the army to shoot them down mercilessly, to cut them
to pieces with the sword and to starve them out.   The
colonial army which often consists of the dregs of the
European population‡ is the most bestial and the most
abominable of all the tools employed by our capitalist
states.   There is hardly a crime which colonial militarism
and tropical madness born of it have not committed.§
The Tippelskirches, Woermanns, Podbielskis, the Leists,
Wehlans, Peters, Arenbergs and Co. are a proof of this
and bear witness to it as regards Germany.   They are
the fruits by which we recognise the essence of colonial
policy, that colonial policy which, under the cloak ‖

---

* Whose colonial expenditure even according to Dernburg's " Memorial "
of October, 1906, is of an overwhelmingly military character in spite of all attempts
to obscure the fact in the balance sheets.

† Since 12th December, 1900, France has a regular colonial army with which
the most horrible experiments are being made : *vide* the *Hamburger Correspondent*,
7th December, 1906 (No. 621), note on . . . p. 3⁰. In Germany they are
busy trying to call such an army into existence.   They are progressing rapidly
in that direction.

‡ *Vide* Peroz, " *France et Japon en Indochine* " ; Famin, " *L'armee coloniale* " ;
E. Reclus' " *Patriotisme et Colonisation* " ; Daeumig's " *Schlachtopfer des Mili-
tarismus*," *Neue Zeit*, 99/00, p. 365 ; on the " *bataillons d'Afri.ue*," p. 369.   In
addition, for Germany, Deputy Roeren on 3rd December, 1906, in the Reichstag.

§ The *disciplinary system* also betrays especially acute forms of brutality.
Concerning the Foreign Legion of France and the *bataillons d'Afri,ue vide*
Daeumig, l.c.

‖ This hypocritical and shameful cloak is now thrown off, with all the cynicism
one could wish for : *vide* article by G. B. in the monthly *Die Deutschen Kolonien*
(October, 1906) and what Strantz said at the conference of the " Pan-German
Society " (September, 1906) : " We don't want to make Christians of the people
in the colonies, they are merely to work for us.   This foolish prattle about
humaneness is simply ridiculous.   German sentimentality has robbed us of such
a man as Peters."   Further, Heinrich Hartert says in the *Tag* of 21st December,
1906 : " It is the duty of the mission . . . to adjust itself to the conditions
as they are " ; but it has " often made itself downright obnoxious *to the trader.*"
This forms the main point of the contention in regard to the colonial policy between
the Centre Party and the Government, and this alone enables one to understand
the fierce attacks delivered by Dernburg, the merchant, on the so-called secondary
government by the (Catholic) Centre.   Here, too, the divine " answer of Alexander"

of spreading Christianity and civilization or of defending the national honour, exploits and deceives with eyes raised to heaven, for the benefit of the capitalists with colonial interests. It murders and violates the defenceless, burns their property, robs and plunders their belongings, thus mocking and bringing disgrace* upon Christianity and civilization. The things perpetrated in India and Tong-king, the Congo State, German South-West Africa and the Philippines eclipse even the stars of a Cortez or of a Pizarro.

PROLETARIAT AND WAR.

When the function of militarism against the enemy abroad is called a national function, it does not mean that it is a function which corresponds to the interests, the welfare and the will of the exploited peoples ruled by capitalism. The proletariat of the whole world has no advantage to expect from this policy which necessitates militarism directed against the enemy abroad; its interests are, in fact, opposed to it in the most striking way. This policy serves directly or indirectly the interests of the exploiting classes of capitalism. It tries with more or less dexterity to pave the way into the world for the recklessly chaotic production and the senseless and murderous competition of Capitalism. In doing this it tramples under foot all the duties of civilization towards the less developed peoples. And in reality it attains nothing save that it insanely endangers the whole fabric of our culture by conjuring up the complications of a world war.

The proletariat, too, welcomes the mighty industrial boom of our day. But it knows that this economic boom could have come about peacefully without the

---

is suited to foreign countries. The *Kreuzzeitung* (29th September, 1906) preaches to *America* as follows : " The extermination of whole tribes of Indians is so inhuman and un-Christian that it cannot, under any circumstances, find justification—especially since it is no case of ' to be or not to be ' for the Americans." Where it is a case of " to be or not to be "—then he who professes love to his neighbour may even " exterminate whole tribes," according to the conception of the colony owning Christians.

    * *Vide* the memorable debates in the German Reichstag on 28th November to 4th December, 1906, in which the " abscess was lanced."

armed hand, without militarism and navalism, without the trident in our fist, and without the bestialities of our economic policy in the colonies, if only it were served by states conducted on a rational basis and working according to an international agreement and in harmony with the duties and interests of Culture. The proletariat knows that our world policy is to a large extent a policy of confusing and overcoming clumsily, by means of violence, the social and political difficulties at home with which the ruling classes see themselves confronted. In short, it is a policy of Bonapartist attempts at deception and leading astray. The proletariat knows that the foes of the workers prefer to cook their soup on the fire of moderate Chauvinism and that already the fear of war unscrupulously worked up by Bismarck in 1887 aptly furthered the interests of the most dangerous reaction. It knows that a recently* exposed little plan of high personages had for its object the filching of the Reichstag electoral rights from the German people while it was in a boisterously patriotic mood "after the home coming of a victorious army." The proletariat knows that this policy tries to turn the economic boom to its advantage, and especially that all the benefit from our colonial policy flows only into the pockets of the employing class, of Capitalism, the hereditary foe of the proletariat. The proletariat knows that the wars which are waged by the ruling classes impose on it heavy sacrifice of life† and property for which it is rewarded with miserable pensions for the disabled, funds in aid of veterans, street organs and kicks of all kinds after it has done the work. The proletariat knows that in every war brutality and baseness are rampant amongst the peoples participating in it and culture is set back for years.‡ The proletariat knows that the fatherland, for which

---

* *Vide* the *Hamburger Nachrichten.* of 3rd November, 1906.
† The loss of human lives in the wars waged from 1799-1904 (apart from the Russo-Japanese war) is estimated at about 15 millions.
‡ *Vide* in this connection Moltke. p. 9, footnote *, and Complete Works, II., p. 288, according to which war is supposed to raise the level of morality and efficiency, and more especially to call forth moral energy.

it must fight, is not its fatherland, that in every country it has only one real foe—the capitalist class which oppresses and exploits it. It knows that all national interests give precedence to the common interests of the international proletariat, and that the international coalition of the exploiters and enslavers must be opposed by the international coalition of the exploited and the enslaved. It knows that the proletariat, to the extent that it might be employed in a war, would be led to fight its own brothers and comrades and, therefore, to fight against its own interests. The class-conscious proletariat remains not only supremely indifferent to the international task of the army and to the whole capitalist policy of expansion, but takes up a position of antagonism to it, clearly understanding why it does so. It is its important task to fight also this class of militarism tooth and nail, and it becomes more and more conscious of this task. This is shown by the international congresses, by the manifestations of fraternity between the German and the French Socialists when the Franco-German war broke out, between the Spanish and American Socialists when the Cuban war broke out, between the Russian and Japanese Socialists when the war of East Asia broke out in 1904. It is also evidenced by the decision arrived at by the Swedish Social-Democrats in 1905 to declare a general strike in the case of a Swedish-Norwegian war ; and further by the parliamentary attitude taken up by the German Social-Democracy towards the war credits in 1870 as well as by the Morocco conflict. It has also been proved by the attitude of the class-conscious proletariat towards an intervention in Russia.

CHARACTERISTICS OF MILITARISM " AGAINST THE ENEMY AT HOME " AND ITS TASK.

Militarism is not only a means of defence against the external enemy ; it has a second task*, which comes

---

* The task of bolstering up the internal order falls to the lot of militarism, not only in the capitalistic, but in all systems of class society.

more and more to the fore as class contradictions become
more marked and as proletarian class-consciousness
keeps growing. Thus the outer form of militarism and
its inner character take a more definite shape : its task
is to uphold the prevailing order of society, to prop up
capitalism and all reaction against the struggle of the
working class for freedom. Militarism manifests itself
here as a mere tool in the class struggle, as a tool in the
hands of the ruling class. It is destined to retard the
development of class-consciousness by working together
with the police and the courts of justice, the school, and
the Church. The task of militarism is, above all, to
secure for a minority, at whatever cost, even against
the enlightened will of the majority of the people,
domination in the state and freedom to exploit.

Thus we are confronted by modern militarism which
wants neither more nor less than the squaring of the
circle, which arms the people against the people itself,
which dares to force the workers (by artificially intro-
ducing by every means the distinction of class according
to age into our social organization) to become oppressors
and enemies, murderers of their own comrades and
friends, of their parents, brothers and sisters and children,
and which compels them to blight their own past and
future. Modern militarism wants to be democratic and
despotic, enlightened and machine-like, nationalist and
antagonistic to the nation at the same time.

All the same one must not forget that militarism is
directed also against the nationalist and even the
religious* enemy at home—in Germany, for instance,
against the Poles,† Alsatians and Danes. It is employed
even in conflicts between the non-proletarian classes.‡
One must not forget that it is a changeable phenomenon§
capable of assuming many forms, and that the Prusso-
German militarism has blossomed out into a special
flower owing to the peculiar semi-absolutist, feudal-
bureaucratic conditions of Germany. This Prusso-

* *Vide* the French struggle for culture during the conflict of December, 1906.
† *Vide* the electoral riot in Upper Silesia in 1903.
‡ *Vide* Fuchsmuehl.
§ *Vide* detail in . . . Chap. V., Part II.

German militarism has all the bad and dangerous qualities of any kind of Capitalist militarism, so that it is an exemplary model of militarism in its present condition, its forms, its methods and effects.

To use Bismarck's words, no one has presumably been able to imitate the Prussian lieutenant ; likewise no one has been able to imitate Prusso-German militarism, which has become not only a state within a state, but actually a state above the state. . . . .

METHODS AND EFFECTS OF MILITARISM.

THE IMMEDIATE OBJECT.

WE now pass to a special examination of the methods and effects of militarism, and in doing so adhere to the exemplary model of the Prussian-German bureaucratic-feudal-capitalist militarism, this worst form of militarism, this state above the state.

Even if it is true that present-day militarism is nothing but a manifestation of our capitalist society, yet it is one which asserts itself more and more as time goes on.

In order to attain its end militarism must turn the army into a handy, pliable, and effective instrument. On the one hand, it must raise it to the highest possible level as to military technique and, on the other hand, as it consists of men and not of machines and presents a living mechanism, it must be filled with the right " spirit."

The first aspect of the thing resolves itself finally into a financial question, which will be discussed later. We shall now occupy ourselves with its second aspect.

Its contents are threefold. Militarism seeks to produce and to further the military spirit, first of all, in the active army, then in those strata which are of importance as the reserve and the *landwehr* from which the army is supplemented in case of mobilization and, finally, in ll the other strata of the population serving as a milieu vhich nurtures those strata of the population which ire to be employed either for militarist or anti-militarist purposes.

MILITARY PEDAGOGY.

EDUCATION OF THE SOLDIER.

The true "military spirit," also called "patriotic spirit" and in Prussia-Germany "spirit of loyalty to the king," means, in short, readiness at all times to strike at the enemy at home or abroad at the word of command. To produce this spirit perfect stupidity or, at least, a very low level of intelligence is needed which makes it possible to drive the masses in the direction dictated by the interests of the "existing order," as one would drive a herd of cattle. The admission of the minister of war, von Einem, that he preferred a soldier who was loyal to the king, even though he were a bad shot, to a soldier whose way of thinking was less correct even though he were a good shot, must surely have come from the bottom of the heart of this representative of German militarism. But here militarism finds itself between the devil and the deep sea. The technique of arms, strategy and tactics now make a great demand upon the intelligence* of the soldier and, therefore, the soldier who is more intelligent, *caeteris paribus*, is also more thorough.† For this reason alone militarism could effect nothing with merely a stupid crowd at the present time. But Capitalism has no use for a stupid crowd, either, because of the economic functions performed by the masses, especially by the proletariat. In order to be able to exploit, to make the biggest possible profits (this is its inevitable life task) Capitalism is forced by a tragic fate to produce systematically on a vast scale amongst its slaves that very intelligence which, as capitalism knows full well, must be the cause of its own death and destruction. All attempts at skilful manœuvring and at a cunning

---

* *Vide* what Caprivi said in the Reichstag on 27th February, 1891 ; von Kaltenbor.-Stachau, minister of war, also said in the Reichstag : "The demands made upon the non-commissioned officers have become much greater in consequence of the new armament, the new regulations *re* training, etc."

† *Vide* the remarks made by the Bavarian General, von Sauer, at the end of October, 1898, before the Politico-Economic Society at Munich.—(Bebel, "No Standing Army," p. 77).

co-operation with the Church and the school to steer the ship of Capitalism between the Scylla of an intelligence so low that it renders exploitation altogether too difficult and turns the proletarian himself into an unsuitable beast of burden, and the Charybdis of an education—necessarily destructive of Capitalism—which increases class-consciousness on all sides and revolutionizes the exploited—all such attempts are bound to fail.

The East-Elbean agricultural workers, according to the noted words of Kroecher, are indeed the most stupid workers, but can still become the best workers for the Junker, be it remembered. They provide militarism on a large scale with material which allows itself to be driven like hordes of slaves at the word of command. Nevertheless this material can be used to advantage only with caution and within certain limits on account of its low level of intelligence, too low even for militarism.

" Our best soldiers are Social-Democrats," one often hears said. This shows how difficult is the task of instilling the true military spirit* into an army under universal military service. Since mere slavish and blind obedience does not suffice and is no longer practicable, militarism is compelled to strengthen the will of the men in a roundabout way in order to create for itself " shooting automatons."† It must shape the will by exerting a moral and a psychological influence or by using means of violence ; it must either coax or force it. The maxim " by fear or favour " is applied here, too.

---

* *Vide* in this connection Caprivi's touching complaint in the Reichstag sitting of 27th February. 1891.

† These " shooting automatons " (*vide* also Corporal Lueck !), too, can become very dangerous, because naturally there may come a day when the mechanism may be set going by an unauthorized person. Then we shall hear the shrieks of the bourgeoisie, which will not only take fright at its own capitalistic resemblance to God, but also at its feudal clique, and will cry out in distress, like the hunter in *Struwwelpeter :* " Oh, help me, good people ! " The bourgeoisie begins to prattle about the " discipline of the German army being raised to such a point that the soldier is incapable of using his judgment," as the *Leipziger Tageblatt* and other papers of its kind did in the Koepenick case. Of course, this does not prevent the bourgeoisie, in the hopelessness of its position, from continuing to offer liberal sacrifices to the moloch of this militarist madness with its " discipline raised to such a point that the soldier is incapable of using his judgment." Another tragic conflict !

The true " spirit " required by militarism in regard to
its function against the enemy abroad is, first represented by Chauvinist stolidity, narrow-mindedness and
self-exaltation, secondly—with regard to its function
against the enemy at home—by a lack of understanding
or even hatred of all progress, of every undertaking
or striving which might threaten the domination of
the ruling class in power for the time being. This is
the channel into which militarism has to lead the
thoughts and feelings of the soldiers when it wishes to
influence by favour those whose class interests are so
opposed to Chauvinism and for whom all progress, in
the light of these class interests, should appear as the
only sensible aim until the downfall of the existing
order of society is brought about. And one should not
ignore the fact that the proletarian of military age,
although he as a rule excels the bourgeois of the same
age as regards independence and political insight, is
not so firm in his class-consciousness.

The system of influencing the soldiers morally and
psychologically is most audacious and cunning. Instead
of separating them according to their social class, they
are classified according to their age, and the system
attempts to create a special class consisting of
proletarians of 20-22 whose ways of thinking and
feeling are to be diametrically opposed to those of the
proletarians in the other and older " classes."

In the first place, the proletarian in uniform is ruthlessly cut off from his comrades and his family. This
is effected by removing him from his native place and,
above all, by shutting him up in barracks,* as is done
systematically in Germany. One can almost call it a
repetition of the Jesuit system of education, a counterpart of the monastic system.

There is next an attempt to continue this isolation as
long as possible. When from the military and the

---

* From the point of view of health this is most serious, and has led in France,
for instance, to the infection of the people with tuberculosis and syphilis in a high
degree. In France five to seven times more cases of tuberculosis are recorded
than in the German army. In a few decades, so someone warns the French,
France will be decimated unless the barrack system is done away with.

technical point of view there is no longer a necessity for a long term of service, this tendency to prolong the isolation is only checked by the financial difficulty. The introduction of the two-year service in Germany* in 1892 is due to this circumstance.

And, lastly, it is a question of making the most of the time allotted to influence the mental outlook of those who are being trained.

As in the case of the Church, all human weaknesses and the senses are enlisted in the service of this military pedagogy. Ambition and vanity are excited, the uniform is proclaimed the best uniform, a soldier's honour is glorified as something especially dignified, and the military caste is trumpeted as being the most important and respected ; and, indeed, it is endowed with many privileges.† They pander to man's love for adornment by cutting the uniforms according to the coarse taste of the lower classes which they wish to attract ; contrary to their purely military purpose they trim the uniforms with tinsel like carnival costumes. All sorts of petty glittering distinctions, decorations, stripes for good shooting, etc., appeal to the same low instinct—the desire for gay apparel and for being looked up to as a distinguished person. And how much of the suffering of soldiers has been soothed by the military bands to which, along with the glittering trimmings on the uniform and the bombastic pomp, is due that widespread popularity—amongst children, fools, servant girls, and the dregs of the proletariat— on which our " magnificent war army " can pride itself. He who has once seen the dubious public which watches parades and the crowd which follows a procession of

---

* _Vide_ Schippel's Handbuch, p. 929.

† Note the state of helplessness of the police (in which they are placed by their superiors) towards the military, especially officers who commit excesses. We must further note the privilege accorded to the military processions to march frequently through the streets in closed ranks of great length, and thus to interfere with the street traffic without any sense or reason ; of course these parades are only dictated by military aesthetics ! A few years ago we saw an instance in Berlin of how the ridiculous pomposity of this pampered frenzy reached the limit and also became a common danger. A section of the fire brigade on its way to a fire was stopped by a military column which marched on, barring its way and not deigning to disturb its beautiful and majestic order by giving place to it. It is true this action was disapproved of later on.

the guard of the royal palace in Berlin will quite understand this. It is well known that this liking for the uniform, felt in certain civilian circles, really constitutes a strong temptation for the unenlightened elements in the army.

All these means are the more effective the lower the intellectual level of the soldiers, and the lower their social position. It is easy to deceive these elements with tinsel and baubles, not merely on account of their small capacity for judgment (one need only imagine an American negro* or an East Prussian menial slave suddenly dressed in the " best " uniform !), but also by reason of the difference between the level of their former civilian life and that of their military position. Thus we have the tragic contradiction that the influence exerted by these means on the intelligent industrial proletarians (for whom they are designed in the first place) is not so great as that exerted on those elements which it seems hardly necessary to influence in this direction, at least for the time being, because they, as things stand, present a sufficiently pliable material for militarism. Nevertheless these means may also help in this case to preserve the spirit agreeable to militarism. The regimental feasts, celebration of the Kaiser's birthday, etc., serve the same end.

When everything has been done to put the soldier into a state of intoxication, to deaden his soul, to fire his imagination and his feelings they begin systematically to play upon his reasoning powers. They start to instruct him and attempt to cram into him a childish representation of the world distorted and whittled down to suit the aims of militarism. Naturally this instruction given mostly by uneducated men without capacity for teaching does not react at all on the intelligent industrial proletarians who are often more intelligent than their instructors. It is an attempt to teach unsuitable subjects or resembles an arrow which rebounds and hits the archer who shot it. This

---

* *Vide* the article in the Berlin *Lokalanzeiger*, No. 638, 1906, on " The American Negro as Soldier."

has not long since been proved to General Liebert by the *Post* and by Max Lorenz (whose perception has been quickened by competition for profit) in regard to anti-Social-Democratic "instruction" of soldiers. Exacting drill, life in the barracks, turning the officer's* and the non-commissioned officer's† uniform (which in many departments of life really seems to be *legibus solutus* and sacrosanct) into a sacred thing, in short, the discipline and control which hold the soldier in iron clamps regarding everything he does or thinks, on duty or off duty, serve to produce the necessary elasticity and obedience of the will. Every individual is so mercilessly bent, tugged at and twisted that the strongest spine is in danger of breaking, and either bends or breaks.‡

The zealous cultivation of the "religious" spirit was demanded by a motion in the budget committee of the Reichstag in February, 1892 (rejected, however, without prejudice). This spiritual training expressly designated as a special object of military education is also here destined to complete the work of military oppression and enslavement.

Instruction and religious belabouring represent at the same time sweetmeats and the whip. The whip is used only sparingly and, for the most part, in a veiled form.

---

* Curious saints, indeed ! Let one call to mind the Bilse case of November, 1903, and the cases of many "little garrisons" *a la* Forbach, the decrees concerning gambling and champagne-drinking, duelling by officers—that *fine fleur* of officer's honour—the stabbing by Bruesewitz (October, 1896) and the shooting by Huessen (*Arenberg*, p. 13 and following), the Harmlos and Ruhstrat affairs, the Bilse and Beyerlein novels portraying life with photographic exactitude, Schlicht's (Count Ba dissin) "First-Class Men," Jesko von Puttkamer, and, last but not least, the Prince Arenberg scandal, which also belongs to this category. The French "small garrison town " Verdun made quite a sensation in the autumn of 1906. Of course, those who worship the uniform look upon all this as a pi iant but amiable weakness in those they worship—who, nevertheless, adhere firmly to the Christian faith. Here again we see manifested the international solidarity of the noblest and the best ! The mutual flagellation by officers of the English Grenadier Guards is an interesting case.—(*La jeunesse socialiste*, March, 1903).

† The non-commissioned officer is "God's representative upon earth."

‡ The most striking proof of this is furnished by the statistics of suicides among soldiers. This, too, is international. According to *official* "statistics" one man in 3700 committed suicide in Germany in 1901 ; in Austria one in about 920. In the Austrian 10th army corps 80 soldiers and 12 officers committed suicide in 1901, and 127 lost their reason and were invalided out in consequence of self-mutilation and maltreatment. During the same period 400 men deserted from the same corps and 725 were condemned to hard labour or rigorous incarceration ! Certainly this state of things is aggravated by the struggle between nationalities.

The sweetmeats used as bait for the formation and filling up of the important permanent *cadres* of the army successfully employed is the system of " capitulation "* with the prospect of premiums† for the non-commissioned officers and of " certificates‡ of provision in civil life."§ This is a very cunning and dangerous arrangement by which militarism contaminates our whole public life, as will be shown later. First and

---

* A soldier in the German army who undertakes to serve a longer term than is prescribed by the law is called a " *capitulant*." A " capitulant " signs a contract undertaking to serve two years extra and receives a premium of 100 marks (£5). Only those soldiers are selected who are suitable to become corporals and non-commissioned officers.— *Trans.*

† Introduced into Germany in 1891 (maximum, 1000 marks). It had been in existence in Saxony and Würtemberg—and a precedent had been established in the Empire by the grant of non-periodic emoluments. It is also in vogue in other countries—for instance, in France—although with little success, where the amounts are much larger (up to 4000 francs). The schools for non-commissioned officers also belong to this category.— *Vide* Vogel von Falkenstein's speech in the Reichstag on 2nd March, 1891.

‡ Caprivi's speech in the Reichstag on 27th February, 1891, is a classical confession of a beautiful capitalist-militarist soul, with its fears and desires, its hopes and aims, and with its methods of pursuing its aims. The speech opens wide the window of such a soul and enables us to take a good look at its inmost secrets. The speech begins with the statement that " only on one condition would they forgo re-introducing the (Anti)-*Socialist law* — namely, that all measures be taken to draw away the ground from beneath the feet of Social-Democracy or that the fight against it be taken up " ; *one of these measures* (a substitute for the Socialist law) *is to be premiums to non-commissioned officers in conjunction with the " certificates of provision in civil life."* Caprivi continued as follows :

" The demands made upon the non-commissioned officers are on the increase because the nation is becoming better educated. The officer in charge can fill his post only if he feels that he is above his subordinates . . .

" If it has now become difficult to enforce discipline it will become more difficult if we have to take up the fight against Social-Democracy ; by a fight I do not mean shooting and stabbing. My memory takes me back to the year 1848. Conditions then were very much better, for at that time ideas had not been produced by long years of schooling, but they had suddenly come to the fore ; therefore the non-commissioned officers of that time had a much easer task when facing the soldiers than now, when they have to face Social-Democracy. (" Hear, hear ! " from the Right.) And to come to an extreme case : we need far better non-commissioned officers for street fights with Social-Democracy than for fighting the enemy. In the face of the enemy the troops can be enthused and induced to sacrifice themselves by patriotism and other lofty feelings. Street fighting and all that follows in its wake is not a factor calculated to raise the sense of dignity of the troops ; they would always feel they were up against their own countrymen.

" The non-commissioned officers can only retain their superiority if we strive to raise them. The allied governments wish to raise the level of the non-commissioned officer class." He further said that it was necessary to turn the non-commissioned officers " into a class whose very existence " would be " bound to the state."

This at the same time portrays the psychology of the *élite* troops.

§ A " certificate of provision in civil life " is a document granted by the military authorities. It testifies that the person in question has served a certain term in the active forces. This entitles him to be provided with civilian work by the Imperial as well as the Federal authorities according to the regulations laid down.— *Trans.*

foremost comes the system of discipline* which is a
whip in the hands of militarism, then comes the military
criminal law which threatens rigorously even the
slightest opposition to the so-called military spirit, and
military justice with its semi-medieval procedure, with
its inhuman, barbarous punishments meted out even
for the slightest insubordination. Excesses committed
by superiors against subordinates are only slightly
punished, and the right of self-defence has been practically
filched from the subordinates. There is nothing more
instructive and nothing that incites one more against
militarism than the perusal of military articles and
military criminal cases.

Here belong also cases of the ill-treatment of soldiers
of which more will be said later. Ill-treatment is not a
method sanctioned by the law, but it is perhaps the most
effective of the coercive disciplinary methods of
militarism.

They attempt to tame men as they tame wild beasts.
They deaden the senses of the recruits, flatter, bribe,
press, imprison, polish, and flog them. Thus grain upon
grain is mixed and kneaded together to serve as mortar
for the mighty edifice of the army, and stone put upon
stone to form a bulwark well calculated to prevent a
revolution.†

---

* Arrest and suspension of food, bed and light, fatigue drill, etc.; also the
barbarous field punishment called "binding on." The Austrian "looking up
in a crooked position" and "binding on," the Belgian cachots and naval "cat-o'-
nine-tails" in international use, and so on, are well known. The horrible methods
of torture applied in the French disciplinary detachments, applied also to "political prisoners," are perhaps not so well remembered. They are : the poucettes,
the menottes, and the crapaudine (vide the illustrated brochure, "Les Bagnes
militaires," published by the "Federation socialiste autonome de (her " in 1902,
speech in the Chamber by Breton ; Georges Darien, "Biribi " (i.e., the collective
name for all the military disciplinary institutions in North Africa), Dubois-Desaulle,
"Sous la Casagne," both published by Stock in Paris). Concerning the com-
pagnies de discipline, the p nitenciers, and the travaur forc s (disciplinary companies, penitentiaries, hard labour) of the French foreign legion and its victims
(vide Daeumig, "Neue Zeit," 99-100, p. 365 and p. 369), just now they are trying
energetically to suppress the "biribi" (Chamber discussions of 8th and 10th
December, 1906).
   The disciplinary flagellation which English officers of the Grenadier Guards
inflict upon one another with a democratic zeal worthy of praise (Jeunesse Socialiste, March, 1903) deserve mention as a curiosity.
   † The result of all these educational methods from the military point of
view has been discussed elsewhere. We will here draw attention to the moral
result, which has caused the bourgeois as well as the anarchist and semi-anarchist
opponents of the army to express themselves with exaggerated cries of indignation.

That these means of luring, punishing and pressure
bear the character of the class struggle is rendered
obvious by the institute for the " one year volunteers."
The " one year volunteer," the son of a bourgeois,
intended for an officer of the reserve, is generally above
the suspicion of having anti-militarist and revolutionary
leanings ; therefore he escapes being sent away from
his native place, being shut up in barracks, instructed
and forced to attend church ; he even escapes a large
part of the exacting drill. It is natural that he is
caught in the mesh of discipline and of military criminal
law only as an exception and is let off lightly. Those
who illtreat the soldiers seldom dare touch them in
spite of their fierce hatred for everything " cultured."
The training of the officers furnishes another striking
proof of this proposition.

The fact that a mass of men work together among
whom the individual has lost his independence is of
supreme importance for military discipline. Each
individual in the army, like a criminal in a galley, is
chained to all the others and is practically incapable of
independent action. The strength of all the others
which is a thousand times greater prevents him by its
overwhelming power from making an independent move.
All the members of this mighty organism, or rather of
this mighty mechanism, are, apart from the hypnotic
influence exerted by those in command, subjected to a
special kind of hypnotism, mass hypnotism whose
influence over enlightened and resolute opponents of
militarism is bound to be nil.

In the domain of educating the soldier some conflict

" The army is the school for crime " (Anatole France) ; " drink, misdemeanour,
and hypocri-y are things taught by barrack life " (Professor Richet). According
to the " manuel du soldat " the term of service is " an apprenticeship in brutality
and villainy " ; " a school for excesses " ; it leads to " moral cowardice, submissiveness, and slavish fear." Indeed, one can scarcely picture to oneself certain
military fetes without patriotic drunkenness which naturally " upholds the state."
The *Leipziger Volkszeitung* of 1st December, 1906, tells of the feasts of military
clubs which Pastor Cæsar calls " drunken brawls." The hygienic result, too,
is by no means pleasing ; as to the French army, *vide* p. 25, note * ; the
sanitary state of the standing armies of England and America, these *democratic*
countries, is quite appalling : the death-rate was much higher than in Germany—
7·13 and 6·18 per thousand in 1906-07 ; according to the report of H. M. O'Reilly,
Surgeon-General of the Army, dysentery and alcoholism are more prevalent
in the American army than anywhere else in the world.

and difficulty arise out of the fact that the purpose of militarism is two-fold. This applies both to training and to equipment. The military training demands more and more imperiously an ever-increasing degree of independence on the part of the soldiers. The soldier requires no independence as a watch-dog of capital, in fact he must not have any ; his qualification for committing suicide should not be taken away from him. In short, war against the external enemy requires men ; war against the enemy at home requires slaves, machines. As regards equipment and armament they cannot dispense with the bright uniforms, glittering buttons and helmets, the flags, parade drills, cavalry attacks, and all the rubbish needed to create the necessary spirit in the struggle against the enemy at home ; in war against the external enemy these things may become downright fatal or simply impossible.*   All the well-intentioned critics of our militarism† who in their innocence merely lay down the criterion for military training have not grasped this tragic conflict whose many aspects cannot be depicted here in extenso.

In this conflict of interests within militarism itself the self-contradiction from which it suffers has the tendency to become more and more acute. It depends each time upon the relation between the political tension at home and abroad which of the two conflicting interests gains the upper hand. One must bear in mind that here lies the germ which will cause militarism to destroy itself.

When the war against the enemy at home in the case of an armed revolution assumes such a forbidding aspect of a purely military-technical character that the decked-out slaves and machines are no longer able to suppress it, then the last hour of the coercive domination by a minority, the capitalist oligarchy, will strike.

---

* When speaking of the struggle against the enemy at home we naturally include the struggle against the spirit of international solidarity, which is disliked by the " militarism directed against the enemy abroad."

† *Vide* " Social-Democracy in the Army," by an Officer (Costenoble, Jena) ; also the material in Bebel's " No Standing Army but a Citizen Army," p. 46 and following, and " Handbook for Social-Democratic Electors," 1903, p. 33 and following.

It is important enough that this military spirit means generally a perversion and confusion of the proletarian class-consciousness, and that militarism serves Capitalism by contaminating with this spirit our whole public life in every direction simultaneously, apart from the purely militarist contamination wrought by it. Militarism does this, for instance, by producing and furthering the spirit of servility in the proletarian who thus submits more readily to economic, social and political exploitation. Militarism also thus retards considerably the proletarian struggle for freedom. We shall have to return to this.

SEMI-OFFICIAL AND SEMI-MILITARY ORGANIZATION OF THE CIVIL POPULATION.

Militarism seeks neither more nor less than to exert on the largest possible scale a strong and lasting influence over the men who belong to the active army. It next seeks to usurp unlimited power over these men, for instance, by means of a system of control, by a wide extension of military jurisdiction, of military courts of honour which are applied* even to officers in the reserve and to those in command. What is here characteristic is the subjection to military jurisdiction of the men called up to appear before the control committees ; the military authorities claim this jurisdiction for the whole day during which a control committee sits and do this openly contravening the law. There is not the least ground for the establishment of such a right ; it is a usurpation pure and simple. To this category further belong the young men's defence clubs and the military clubs with their semi-official and semi-military management, with their aping of the military dress, tomfoolery and feasting. What is of great importance in this domain of militarist activity is the mischief done by the officers of the reserve who bring the military caste spirit into civil life and perpetuate it. Still

---

* *Vide* in this connection the well-known Gaedke case, in which the Prussian Court of Appeal legally stamped the astounding aspirations of militarism.

C

greater mischief is done in regard to the higher civilian officials of the state and communal administration as well as those of justice and of the educational system* who are subjected almost without exception to military discipline, to the military spirit, to the whole militarist conception of life. Thus every awkward opposition movement which was not entirely impossible is cut short in advance. In this way the submissiveness of the civil executive is secured in conjunction with the system of " military expectants,"† which plays the same *role* for the subalterns and the lower officials. Thus provision is made that the trees of class justice and the system of class education grow high into the sky of militarism whereas the trees of self-government‡ are thoroughly pruned. We cannot ignore the fact that officers on active service and in the reserve are expressly forbidden to engage in writing. This, together with the highly instructive Gaedke case, is the strongest proof that militarism strives ruthlessly to subjugate spiritually and control from a central station everything that comes anywhere within its reach. It also indicates its tendency to continuously extend its sphere of influence by legal or illegal means, and its insatiable craving for power.

OTHER MILITARY INFLUENCES ON THE CIVIL POPULATION.

A still more important fruit of the militarist craving for expansion than even the mischief done by the officers of the reserve is the wretched system of " military expectants." Apart from its purely military aim this

---

* Also many members of the doctors' profession ; as to the results *vide*, for instance, the note in the *Vorwaerts* of 17th January, 1894. It is not the military doctors of the reserve alone who are subject to this pressure ; they bring this pressure to bear on the professional organizations and in this way on the non-military doctors.

† " *Military expectants* " are persons in Germany who by long service or through having been invalided out of the army acquire the right to be employed in civil employment. They receive " *certificates of provision in civil life* " which entitle them to work in certain occupations. These " military expectants " are to comprise 50 per cent. in certain occupations and they have precedence over civilians.— *Trans.*

‡ The bold adventure of Voigt, the " Captain " of Koepenick, the ingenious cobbler and convict, has also been characterized as a warning by the Liberals.

system also serves the aim of sending forth a following of faithful and enthusiastic representatives and advocates of the militarist spirit into all the branches of the state and communal administration. At the same time the reliability and readiness* of the bureaucratic apparatus which serves capitalism is thus to be secured and the " proper " way of thinking " ready to uphold the state " is to be carried among the mass of the people who are in especial " need of education." This " educational " aim of the " certificate of provision in civil life " was acknowledged with splendid unanimity and frankness in the discussions about premiums for non-commissioned officers by Caprivi, the Imperial Chancellor, as well as by the representatives of the ruling classes in February, 1891, in the German Reichstag. So this is the state-upholding ideal of our popular education, which, as luck would have it, has become embodied in the non-commissioned officer in a roundabout way after the corporal (its previous bearer) had had to leave the desk.

The results of education are, however, quite meagre. And the poor devil of a " military expectant " occupying the post of a lower official is very badly paid. And it may, in the long run, become impossible to procure even a German non-commissioned officer *pour le roi de Prusse.*† It is the eternal problem of trying to buy out the revolution !

It must be further mentioned in this connection that the means by which the military enthusiasm of the soldiers is produced and maintained, viz., by all the tinsel and show of uniform and decorations, are at the same time employed to influence in favour of militarism the population outside its scope and the strata from which the army is recruited, which supply it with the tinsel, which have to bear its cost and are in " danger " of succumbing to the enemy at home. Haldane, the English war minister, during his visit to Prussia in the autumn of 1906, was quick to notice this. He expressed

---

* Both in the figurative and the literal sense of the word !— *Vide* p. 48.
† In Germany there exists a kind of union of these officials, the " Bund deutscher Militaeranwaerter " (Union of " Military Expectants ").

himself thus : " A valuable phenomenon which accompanies militarism is that through coming in closer touch with the army and the preparations for war the nation learns sober-mindedness and loyalty."*

Militarism possesses a means of quite a different type for spreading its spirit. Militarism effects it in its capacity *as a consumer and a producer*, and by influencing great state economic concerns of strategic importance.

A whole host of manufacturers, artisans and merchants with their employees subsists on the army. They participate in the production and transport of articles necessary for equipping, lodging and maintaining the army, and all articles used by the soldiers. These hangers-on of the army sometimes actually impress their stamp upon the whole public life, especially of the smaller garrison towns ; the more powerful of them rule like princes over great communities and help to play first fiddle in the state, in the Empire. They wield their influence, thanks to militarism, which permits them to exploit it with astounding patience and allows its ears to be boxed. They repay militarism (one hand washes the other) by becoming its zealous advocates ; their capitalist interest alone inciting them to do this. Who does not know the names : Krupp, Stumm, Ehrhardt, Loewe, Woermann, Tippelskirch, Nobel, the Powder Ring, etc. ? Who does not know of Krupp's profits from armour plate, of the Tippelskirch profits and the bribes that go with them, the inflated Woermann freight and demurrage charges and the net gains of the Powder Ring amounting to 100 and 150 per cent., which have relieved the German treasury of many a million ? †
The swindling of the purveyors, especially in Austria, caused a great sensation.‡ And each campaign means a swindler's golden harvest for the pack of parasites, and that not only in Russia.§ These great lords reward

* *Vide* the *Lokalanzeiger*, No. 496, 1906.
† *Vide* Feuchter, " The Powder Ring," 1896, pp. 25 and 30.
‡ Details in " Lustig ist's Soldatenleben," p. 51.
§ Where the Gurko-Lidvalls, the last stragglers of the crowd of vultures connected with the war in Eastern Asia, caused a great sensation at the end of 1906.

militarism in the most Christian way by continuing to rob it or rather the people. They pour the holy ghost of militarism over " their " workmen and everything that is dependent on them, and they wage a ruthless war against revolution. Of course the real material interest neither of these workmen nor of the bulk of the petty army purveyors is bound up with the army. In countries where there is no standing army trade and industry are in a no less flourishing condition than in those states which possess a standing army. The persons engaged in military production would be economically no worse off if there were no army. However, for the most part they do not see beyond the end of their own noses and succumb easily to the strenuous militarist influence, so that a counter-revolution meets with great difficulties.

As an employer in the large economic concerns (in the commissariat, in the preserve factories, in the clothing departments, repair depôts, arms and munition factories, dockyards, etc.) militarism most readily and without exception delivers its employees (on 31st October, 1904, the German army and navy administration employed a total of 54,723 persons* in the works under the direct control of the state) to the reactionary patriotic demagogy, such as the Imperial Union against Social-Democracy. Militarism also attempts systematically to develop the patriotic militarist spirit in the most ruthless manner by means of baits, such as : titles, decorations, arrangement of fêtes similar to those of the military clubs and of impossible pensions, by even slandering the trade unions and by a real barrack discipline.† The military workshops more than any

---

* Naval administration, 18,939 ; Prussian army administration, exclusive of the Ordnance department, 11,199 ; Prussian Ordnance department, 16,825 ; Bavarian army administration, 4,632 ; Saxon army administration, 2,754 ; Wurtemberg army administration, 374.—(*Vide* printed documents of the Reichstag, 1905-1906, No. 144).

† In the case connected with the theft of arms in Posen in the winter of 1906, the accused, a factory hand at Spandau, stated again and again that he had to obey Lieutenant Poppe, the thief, who "as an officer" was "to a certain extent his superior " ; thus they had been taught. Poppe was not employed in the works to which the accused belonged. The genuine officer's uniform assisted him in his shady doings among the civilian population just as the unauthorised uniform had assisted the captain of Koepenick.

other state workshops present the most difficult field
for enlightening the proletariat. Of course, the influence
which is antagonistic to Labour has its limits, and the
military administration cherishes no illusions concerning
the successes of the Social-Democrats achieved, especially
amongst the " Imperial " dock workers. All threats,
some of which are very childish, to close down the
military workshops if the Social-Democratic vote
amongst the workmen should continue to increase (a
manœuvre employed, for instance, in the election of
1903 at Spandau) are powerless to hinder the development of the class-consciousness as long as militarism
continues to pay its workmen niggardly wages and thus
attract them to the ranks of Social-Democracy. One
need only recall the frequent agitation for higher wages
amongst the workmen of the royal factories, and the
countless conflicts which they have with the military
administration* to become less pessimistic.

The railways, post and telegraph are institutions of
immense strategical importance and as much in a war
against the enemy at home as against the enemy abroad.
These indispensable factors of strategical importance
can be rendered useless to militarism by a strike which
may lead to a complete breakdown of the military
organism. This explains why militarism tries so hard
to instil its spirit into the officials and workmen's
organizations in connection with the means of communication and with the productive concerns which
are allied to them (railway shops, coach factories,
etc.). And in what an unscrupulous way this endeavour
is pursued, even apart from the system of the " military
expectants," is shown by the subjection of these
employees to military law which has been achieved in
many states. We also see it if we take a cursory view
of the political position of these employees in the

* The struggles in the workshops at Spandau which come up in the Reichstag
every year are well known. Concerning the clothing department of the Berlin
corps, *vide* the *Fachzeitung der Schneider* of 25th August, 1906 ; concerning the
French naval arsenals at Brest, Lorient, Cherbourg, Rochefort, and Toulon, *vide*
the *Temps Nouveaux* of 11th November, 1905. At the present moment (December, 1906) there is a strong movement afoot among the arsenal workers of Toulon ;
one cannot foresee how it will end.

militarist states where they are deprived of the right to form trade unions by administrative order (this is the case in Germany and in France*) or by means of special laws (as, for instance, in Italy, Holland and Russia†). Of course, we must overlook the fact that the capitalist state, apart from these militarist interests, has quite a general interest that the employees of the systems of communication should not succumb to aspirations " antagonistic to the state." But this endeavour must needs remain unsuccessful in the long run even if it puts difficulties in the way of the Labour movement. It is shattered by the low wages and by the *de facto* proletarian position of the employees of the systems of communications.

MILITARISM AS MACHIAVELIANISM AND AS A POLITICAL REGULATOR.

Accordingly militarism makes its appearance first as the army itself, then as a system projected beyond the army which penetrates the whole society by a network of militarist and semi-militarist institutions (the system of control, courts of honour, prohibition to engage in writing, the class of the officers of the reserve, " certificates of provision in civil life," militarization of the bureaucratic apparatus which is due, in the first place, to the mischief caused by the class of the officers of the reserve and to the wretched system of " military expectancy," young men's defence clubs, military clubs, and so on). Further, militarism makes its appearance as a system which *saturates the whole public and private life of our people with the militarist spirit.* The Church, the school, and the tendency of a cheap art, further the press, a miserable mob of venal *litterateurs* and the social nimbus *which surrounds* " our glorious war army " *like a halo*—all these work together in a tenacious and cunning manner. Militarism along with the Catholic

---

* The French government has formally tried to justify these measures by drawing attention to the anti-militarist propaganda : the *Temps Nouveaux*, etc.

† Law of 2nd December, 1905 ; *vide* in this connection the *Leipziger Volks-zeitung*, 14th December, 1906.

Church is the worst Machiavelianism in the world's history and the most Machiavelian of all the Machiavelianisms of Capitalism.

The oft-mentioned clever stroke of the cobbler of Koepenick presents a lesson in the catechism of militarist methods of education and their results ; the most sublime point in this catechism is that the whole of the bourgeois society is actually looking upon the officer's uniform as sacred. In the examination held by this convict which lasted six hours our army, our bureaucratic apparatus and allegiance to Prussia were put to a test. All the pupils passed it so brilliantly that it made their teachers' hair stand on end when they saw what the quintessence of their pedagogy amounted to. No hat of Gessler's has been greeted with such submissive obedience and self-degradation as the hat of the immortal captain of Koepenick, no sacred cloak of Trier has found so many credulous devotees as his uniform. The great effect of this classic satire lies in the fact that it has run to death the principles of militarist pedagogy. Militarism itself should have been laughed out of court by the jeering scorn and ridicule of the world if the militarism of the bourgeois society (which now for a moment finds itself in the *role* of a sorcerer's apprentice) were not as necessary as our daily bread and as the air we breathe. Capitalism and its mighty steward militarism are not in love with one another : they rather fear and hate each other and they have many a reason for that. They regard each other—for this steward has become so independent—as a necessary evil ; and again there are many reasons for this. And thus the lesson of Koepenick which cannot be followed by bourgeois society will merely remain a powerful means of agitation in the hands of Social-Democracy* and of anti-militarism.

* It is delightful to see the *Kreuzzeitung* wriggle about in the trap. In its hopeless plight it tries to turn the point by making out that Social-Democracy is in a plight : that the Koepenick stroke had prematurely disclosed to the world the plans Social-Democracy had made for the event of a revolution, and that they had now been frustrated. What is especially absurd about all this prattle prompted by mortal fear is the illusion th t such plans could ever be frustrated under the capitalist order, and that the Knights of the *Kreuzzeitung* would ever move a finger in such a hopeless attempt. "Thank God, we can still rely on the military !" All said and done, this was an honest sigh of relief heaved by our bourgeois Philistines after the bold stroke at Koepenick.

These thrive the better, the more militarism brings matters to a head.

What the " Captain " of Koepenick did for militarism in practice was accomplished as cleverly in the domain of theory by the invaluable Gustav Tuch at the end of the 'eighties. In his thick, dusty old volume, " The Extended Military State in its Social Significance," he sketched a future society in which militarism, the only true " national and civilized Socialism," was the central sun which lighted, warmed and directed everything, and was the heart and soul of everything. In this volume society is turned into a single barrack ; the barrack is the elementary school, the university and the factory for manufacturing patriotic opinions, and the army is an all-embracing organization of strike-breakers. This rapturous hallucination of a millennium of militarism was in reality only methodical madness. But the fact that it was *methodical* madness which had thought out to the utmost militarist aims and methods freeing them from every idea that might blur them, gives it a symptomatic meaning.*

At least in one respect, which is of a dominant character, militarism has already become to-day the central sun, as will be shown later in more detail, around which revolves the solar system of class legislation, bureaucratism, police administration, class justice, and of clericalism of all shades. It is the final regulator, now secret, now open, of all class politics, of the tactics in the class struggle not only of the capitalist classes, but also of the proletariat, and as much in its trade union organization as in its political organization.

---

* *Vide* K. Kautsky, *Neue Zeit*, 1887, p. 331.

Chapter IV.

PARTICULARS OF SOME OF THE CHIEF SINS OF MILITARISM.

Ill-treatment of Soldiers, or Militarism as a Penitent yet Incorrigible Sinner.

Two Contradictory Situations.

THE militarists are no fools. This is proved by the educational system worked out with extreme cunning. They show considerable skill in their speculation concerning the psychology of the masses. The standing army of Frederick, consisting of hired soldiers and the dregs of the population could be held together by means of exacting drill and blows for the performance of its tasks which were of a more mechanical character. This no longer applies to our army which is drawn from our whole population with its higher level of intelligence and morality ; the army is built upon the principle of citizen duty and it makes greater demands upon the individual. This was at once recognized* by Scharnhorst and Gneisenau whose army organization was begun with the announcement that corporal punishment was abolished. Nevertheless abuse, blows and all kinds of refined and horrible methods of ill-treatment belong to the stock-in-trade of the militarist educational system of to-day, as has been shown.

The attitude taken on the militarist side towards ill-treatment of soldiers is not determined by ethics, culture, humaneness, justice, Christianity and similar fine things, but by purely Jesuitical considerations of expediency.

It has not yet by a long way become common know-

---

* *Vide* the highly interesting although illusory " Regulations as to military punishments."

42

ledge* that this ill-treatment is a secret underground menace which threatens the discipline and even the " spirit " of the army.† The recruits and the troublesome soldiers being " jeered at and humbled " by the old soldiers, the vulgar expressions and the coarse abuse of all kinds, as well as a considerable amount of cuffing, prodding and beating, etc., of " throwing the men up in the air and letting them fall down," of " dragging the men along the ground till they lose consciousness," is even to-day approved in their hearts without any scruples by the majority of the non-commissioned officers and even officers (who have become estranged and antagonistic to the people and trained to be narrow-minded politicians in miniature who employ violence) ; in fact, these things are looked upon as indispensable. If one attempts to struggle against these excesses one meets with resolute passive resistance from the first. One can hear every day—not openly but on the quiet— how the superiors characterize the demand that " the fellows " be treated in a way which is commensurate with human dignity as stupid humanitarian prattle. The army service is a harsh service. But even if one has come to recognize the underground menace—disciplinary ill-treatment which is at work below the surface—one finds oneself again in one of those contradictory situations into which a coercive system, as it does not follow the path of natural development, must land at every step ; some of these contradictory situations we have already brought to light. The method of ill-treatment, as will be shown in more detail, is an indispensable auxiliary of the open drill ; a discipline prompted by free will remains unattainable for Capital.

---

* The mass of deserters and of those liable to serve but who evade military service serves, *inter alia*, as a remote guide. 15,000 German deserters lost their lives during the first 30 years of the glorious Empire in the French colonial army alone, whilst the bloody battle of Vionville claimed only 16,000 dead and wounded — *Vide* Daeumig, p. 371, etc.

† The order by Manteuffel, dated 18th April, 1885, shows insight, for it says, among other things : " Abuse injures and destroys one's sense of honour, and an officer who abuses his subordinates wallows in his own blood : for one cannot rely either on the loyalty or bravery of him who allows himself to be abused." " In a word, as the superiors, from the general down to the lieutenant treat their subordinates so they are."

ism.   Ill-treatment serves, in spite of all scruples and
regret—we repeat, not officially but semi-officially—as
an indispensable though illegal method of militarist
education.

Militarists have a bad conscience, apart from this
scruple, since they have been caught, that is to say,
since the ruthless Social-Democratic criticism has been
levelled at the military organization and now that even
wide strata of the middle class begin to recoil from this
militarist morality.   Militarism had to bear with set
teeth the fact that it (militarism) was not being staged
and commanded by the supreme war-lord, but that its
material existence was dependent, above all, on the
people's representatives looked down upon with
contempt, upon the Reichstag in which sit even the
representatives of the rabble ; in short, is dependent
upon the " scoundrels." Militarism had to put up
with having its nakedness mercilessly exposed time after
time under the protection of the Reichstag immunity.
Militarism saw itself obliged, suppressing its rage, to
keep the men of low birth, the " Reichstag fellows,"
and the despised and scorned public opinion in a good
mood.   It was a case of not putting the military piety
of the bourgeoisie (which was ready to grant military
credits for every possible object, but which tried not
infrequently, especially in times of financial stress, to
kick against the pricks) to too severe a test and to ease
its position as much as possible in regard to its electors,
who, according to their mode of life for the most part
belong to the anti-militarist classes and who, when they
recognize their class position would go over to Social-
Democracy.   It was necessary to deprive Social-
Democratic agitation of its most effective weapons, so
they next followed the tactics of hushing up and of
glossing matters over.   The proceedings of the military
courts took place in secret, " no ray of light penetrated
the darkness of their heart."   If any ray did penetrate
they denied, disputed and embellished things with all
their might.   Yet the torch of Social-Democracy shed
more and more light even behind the barrack walls and

through the bars of military prisons and fortresses. The military debates in the German Reichstag in the 'eighties and 'nineties of the past century represent a hard and passionate fight for the recognition of the fact that the barrack horrors were not a manifestation which made their appearance but seldom and in iso ated cases, but that they were a regular, frequent, and to a certain extent an organic, constitutional manifestation of militarism. This fight was rendered good service by the fact that the proceedings of the military courts in other states were conducted in public, which made it easier to supply incontestable proofs that military ill-treatment was a regular property of militarism, even of the republican militarism of France, of Belgian militarism, and to an ever increasing extent of the militarism of the Swiss militia. Social-Democratic criticism scored a victory mainly owing to the impression created by the decrees of Prince George of Saxony (8th June, 1891)* and of the Bavarian ministry of war (of 13th December, 1891) (both published in *Vorwaerts* at the beginning of 1892), as well as the Reichstag debates which lasted from 15th to 17th February, 1892. The usual " considerations " and wrangling of every sort resulted finally in 1898 in the reform of our military criminal procedure. The reform still made it possible on a large scale to hang the cloak of Christian love over the frightful secrets of the barracks by means of excluding publicity. In spite of all the precautions taken, and in spite of the measures (much commented upon) taken by the judges who tried Bilse the reform soon brought to light such a cloudburst of horrible cases of ill-treatment that all objections to Social-Democratic criticism were simply brushed aside and the torturing of soldiers was recognized almost everywhere, even if unwillingly, as a

---

* They speak here of "conditions which are serious in a high degree," of " refined torture," of " an efflux of brutality and degeneracy " which is " hardly credible " with such officers in charge and which the system of control in practice should have been rendered " scarcely possible," it was thought. On 8th February, 1895, *Vorwaerts* published an Imperial decree (also applicable to this case) to the generals in command, dated 6th February, 1890. The decrees of Scharnhorst-Gneisenau (after Jena) and Manteuffel (18th April, 1885), also the decree of the hereditary prince of Meiningen, have a bearing on another matter,

standing institution of militarism which upholds the
state. They tried, not altogether honestly, to come to
grips with this awe-inspiring institution which favoured
Social-Democratic agitation. Even if they did not
believe they would achieve success they wanted to
create the impression that they were not satisfied with
this manifestation and were ready to do their best to
remove it. They began to prosecute the torturers of
soldiers with certain thoroughness, but the fight against
ill-treatment by the military is, for militarism, of less
importance than its interest in maintaining military
discipline and in making the people ready to bear arms
in the fight against their own national and international
interests. Let us put the sentences passed on the
torturers of soldiers of the commonest kind side by side
with the sentences which are passed on soldiers very
often for minor offences, which are committed in excitement or in a state of drunkenness against their superiors
almost every day. On the one hand, the slightest
misdemeanours against the holy ghost of militarism are
punished in a blood-thirsty and draconic way ; on the
other hand, in cases of soldiers being unjustly and
cruelly treated, comparative indulgence and connivance
are shown in spite of the gravity of the offence. So
that it is natural that the fight of military justice against
military ill-treatment, which goes hand in hand with
a pitiless suppression of every sign which indicates that
the consciousness of independence or of equal rights
is awakening in the subordinates, yields practically no
results. The case of the hereditary prince of Saxe-
Meiningen explains everything. He had the courage to
appeal to his men to support the fight against ill-
treatment ; in fact, to make it their business to support
it in order to get to the root of the evil with more
determination than usual. But owing to this bold step
the Prince was soon forced to retire from the service.*
This case throws a lurid light upon the falsity and

---

* *Vide*, for instance, the case of the unfortunate Rueckenbrodt, in which
a rope-like packing of asbestos covered with wire played a horrible part. With
biting irony it was named the "military educator" by the torturers of soldiers.
—(*Vorwaerts*, 25th September, 1906,)

futility of the official struggle with cases of military ill-treatment.

The booklet, " Opfer der Kaserne " (" Victims of the Barracks ") by our comrade Rudolf Kraff , a former Bavarian officer, contains valuable material ; it is put together with expert skill and could have only been done by one who had lived through it himself. The regular compilation by our Party press of cases of ill-treatment of soldiers — not only in the army but also in the navy*—which had come up for trial and had been made public during certain periods furnish an overwhelming mass of material. Unfortunately, it has not yet been put into shape.† This is an important and useful task for someone to perform.

Owing to our fundamental principles we cherish no illusions concerning militarism. The Scharnhorst decree concerning military punishments expresses the following opinion : " Experience teaches us that recruits can be taught to drill without blows. An officer who thinks this is impracticable lacks either the necessary ability to teach or a clear conception of what constitutes teaching." This is, of course, theoretically true, but it was too far in advance of its time to be put into practice. Military ill-treatment of soldiers has its origin in the inner essence of capitalist militarism. The human material is, for the most part, mentally and also to a great extent physically, not capable of meeting the military demands, especially that of the parade drill. More and more young men enter the army whose life conception is antagonistic and dangerous to the military spirit. It is necessary to tear out to a certain extent the former soul of these " fellows " and

---

* *Vide* the *Frankfurter Zeitung* of 6th April, 1903, the Reichstag discussions cf 4th and 8th March, 1904, especially the speeches by the deputies Bebel, Lede-bour, and Mueller-Meiningen ; *vide* also *Vorwaerts* of 6th, 13th, 14th, and 21st May, 1903. Further, the cabinet order re-printed in the *Army Gazette* of 29th April, 1903, which emphasizes the fact that it is not the soldiers' *duty* to lodge complaints, but only that they have the *right* to complain. Also the *Military Weekly* of 29th May, 1903, according to which the fact that the hereditary prince had been thrown over and obliged to retire had caused " a most painful sensation." In what quarters ?

† There is something, too, in " Prinz Arenberg und die Arenberge," p. 15 and following, about " aristocrats who ill-treat soldiers."

to implant a fresh patriotic soul, loyal to the king.
All these problems cannot be solved even by the most
skilful teacher, let alone the kind of instructors whom
militarism has at its disposal ; even in this respect
militarism has to be more economical than it likes to be.*

And these military instructors have no assured
existence. They are entirely dependent upon the
goodwill and the arbitrariness of their superiors ; they
may expect to be dismissed any time when they cease
to perform their main task which is to fashion the
soldiers after the image of militarism. It is an excellent
means of making the whole apparatus of military
superiors (officers and non-commissioned officers) extremely pliable in the hands of the authority in command.
One can understand that such superiors drill men with
a nervous ruthlessness which is soon reduced to : " If
you do not carry out my wishes I will use violence."
That violence which is finally employed in the form
of ill-treatment by the superiors who have absolute
power, even over the lives of their subordinates who
are subjected to them unconditionally, is a natural and
humanly necessary corollary ; the fresh baked Japanese
militarism got itself very quickly involved in it.†
Militarism has also landed itself in this contradictory
situation.

It is true that the causes of such " coarse pleasures "
are not everywhere the same. The degree of education
of the people, above all, exerts a strong modifying
influence.‡ One need not wonder that even French
colonial militarism contrasts favourably with the
militarism of the Prusso-German fatherland.§

This form of applying violence as a disciplinary
measure, due to the necessity inherent in the system,

---

* On 27th February, 1891, Caprivi explained with regard to the ill-treatment
of soldiers : "The educated non-commissioned officer is of more value to us
than the brutal one, because the former seldom allows himself to be carried away
by his temperament, even though he be angered." But where are the educated
non-commissioned officers to be got from without kidnapping them ?

† Vide, for instance, the Brandenburger Zeitung of 8th December, 1906.

‡ Germany recognizes no line of demarcation here formed by the river Main.
In the domain of the ill-treatment of soldiers, at least, German unity and concord
have been realized.

§ Vide Dauemig, p. 370, and other sources.

affords us an excellent means of fighting militarism in a thorough way and with success. It is a means of whipping up against militarism ever greater masses of the people and of spreading class-consciousness among those strata which are not yet access ble to it or to which access otherwise would be more difficult. Military ill-treatment in conjunction with militarist class justice is one of the most rousing manifestations of capitalist lack of culture. Military ill-treatment being at the same time an underground menace to the military discipline is the most effective weapon in the proletariat's fight for freedom. This sin of capitalism turns against itself with double force. And the sinner may be ever so penitent, either honestly downcast in his helplessness, or penitent after the style of a Brer Fox, yet we must not allow these weapons to be snatched from us, for in spite of sackcloth and ashes this penitent sinner is incorrigible.

COST OF MILITARISM, OR " LA DOULOUREUSE."
ANOTHER CONTRADICTORY SITUATION.

Historical materialism, the teaching of dialectical evolution, is the teaching of the immanent necessity of retaliation. Every class society is doomed to commit suicide, every class society is a force which always wants what is bad and does what is good. Every class society is doomed to destruction by the inherited sin of its class character. Whether it wants it or not, every class society must produce the Oedipus who will one day destroy it and, unlike the legendary Theban, it will be fully conscious of the fact that it is committing patricide ; this applies in any case to the capitalist social order and to the proletariat. Certainly the ruling class of capitalism would like to look after its material interests quite unperturbed. But this imperturbability is not tolerated either by capitalist competition, national or international, nor does it correspond for any length of time to the taste of those out of whose hides capitalism cuts thongs. So capitalism sets up a terrible stronghold of coercive domination, bristling with weapons, to protect wage slavery and the holy of holies of profit. But though militarism is a life necessity for capitalism it is not by any means enamoured of the enormous cost of it ; on the contrary, this cost is in reality very disagreeable to it. But as to-day it is no longer possible, according to the old prescription of Cadmus, to saw teeth and to see armed soldiers spring up out of the ground, there remains nothing to be done save to put up with the moloch nature of militarism and to feed its insatiable greed.

The budget discussions which take place in the parliaments every year show how much pain is caused to the ruling classes by this property of militarism. Capitalism which produces the surplus value can again be hit in its fundamentally weak spot, viz., finance. The costliness of militarism is the only thing which keeps it within bounds of any sort, at least in so far as the cost has to be borne by the bourgeoisie itself. It is true, the morality of the profiteers seeks a convenient and despicable way out of the difficulty and succeeds in finding it : they pile the greatest part, or at least a large part, of the military burdens on the shoulders of those strata of the population which are not only the weakest, but to oppress and to torment which militarism has chiefly been set on foot. The capitalist classes, like the ruling classes of other social systems, make use of their coercive domination based upon the exploitation of the proletariat for the following purpose : the oppressed and exploited classes are not only compelled to make their own chains, but even to pay for them as far as possible. It does not suffice that the sons of the people are turned into the torturers of the people, but even the pay of these torturers is, as much as possible, wrung from the sweat and blood of the people. And even if the provoking action of this bloody stroke of chicanery is perceived here and there, capitalism remains true unto death to its faith—the faith in the golden calf.

It is true that by throwing the military burdens on to the shoulders of the poorer classes the degree is lowered to which these classes can be exploited. But no sophistry can do away with the fact, so this, too, helps to set capitalism (which is so fond of exploiting) against moloch.

Militarism weighs like lead on our whole life ; but it is especially an *economic* weight, an incubus under which our economic life groans, a vampire which constantly, year after year, sucks its blood by withdrawing from the work of production and culture the best strength of a nation, and by incurring insane direct expenditure. In *Germany* at present about 655,000* of the strongest men best capable of engaging in production—mostly of 20-22 years of age—are permanently withdrawn from work. In *Germany* the military and naval expenditure which goes up in leaps and bounds amounts to over 1300 million marks† (£65,000,000), or to 1⅓ milliards, roughly, for the year 1906-7, for instance. This includes the expenditure on the colonies but not the supplementary expenditure. The expenditure of the *other military states* is not less heavy in comparison,‡ and even the military expenditure of the more favoured states, such as the American Union, England (1321 million marks— £66,000, oo—on the army and the navy in 1904-5), Belgium and Switzerland, is so enormous that it forms the chief item in the state budget. There is a tendency for the expenditure to increase everywhere ; the upgrade movement is checked only by the utmost capacity to meet the expenditure having been reached.

The following compilation of the *Nouveau Manuel du Soldat* is very good :

" In 1899 Europe had a military budget of
Francs 7,184,321,093 (£287,372,844).
There were employed in a military capacity :
4,169,321 men.

---

* 1906-7 : 614,362 men in the standing army ; 1905-6 : 40,672 men in the navy.

† Each soldier fighting in German South-West Africa cost the German Empire 9,500 marks (£475) a year.

‡ In France, for instance, 1,101,260,000 francs (£44,050,400) in 1905. Since 1870 France has expended nearly 40 milliard francs (£160,000,000) for military purposes (exclusive of the colonies !).

If the men were working they could earn daily (at the rate of 3 francs a day per man) :

Francs 12,507,963 (£500,318).

Further, Europe needed for military purposes :

710,342 horses,

which could produce daily at the rate of 2 francs a day per horse :

Francs 1,420,684 (£56,827).

This added to the francs 12,507,963 amounts to francs 13,928,647 (£557,145). If we multiply this amount by 300 and add to it the budget, it shows a loss in productive values amounting to :

Francs 11,362,915,913 (£454,516,344).

" But from 1899-1906/1907 Germany's military budget alone has risen from about 920 million marks (£46,000,000) to about 1300 million marks (£65,000,000), or more than 40 per cent. The total military expenditure of Europe would probably now amount to about :

Francs 13,000,000,000 (£520,000,000),

without including the cost of the Russo-Japanese war. This represents about 13 per cent. of the foreign trade of the world ; indeed, it is a way of doing business which must end in bankruptcy."

As in the Russian Baltic Provinces the military suppression of the revolutionary movement was for a long time transferred to the barons who had been hit by the revolution, so in America the unlimited possibility has been created of entrusting to the capitalist class, even in times of peace, the maintenance of capitalist order to a certain extent. This is done by means of the Pinkertons, who have straightway become a legal institution employed in the class struggle. This institution, like the Belgian form of National Guard, has, at any rate, the advantage that it modifies* the phenomena which accompany militarism (ill-treatment of soldiers, the expenditure, etc.) and are disliked by the bourgeoisie itself. Thus the enemy of capitalist society is partially deprived of highly effective propa-

---

* But even in the U.S.A. the war and naval departments alone swallowed $240,000,000 out of a total of $720,000,000 budgetted for,

ganda matter. But this way out of the difficulty—
which is nothing but pleasing to the proletariat—as a
rule is barred to the capitalist states, as has been said
before. As far as we can see ahead they are prevented
from adopting a system of militia which, from the
economic point of view, would be less burdensome,
by the political task of the army at home, the function
it performs in the class struggle. In fact, this function
betrays a striking tendency to do away with the existing
forces of militia.

If one compares the total expenditure of the *German
Empire* which amounted to 2,397,324,000 (£119,866,200)
for 1906-7 with the portion which is spent on the army
and the navy one sees that all the other items play the
part of satellites as opposed to this gigantic portion :
that the whole system of taxation, the whole financial
policy centres round the military budget " like the
multitude of stars around the sun."

So that militarism becomes a dangerous drag, often
even the gravedigger of that progress of culture which
per se might be in the interest of the social order of
to-day. The school, art and science, public hygiene,
the system of communications : all these are treated in
the most niggardly way because, to use a well-known
phrase, moloch's greed leaves nothing over for the tasks
of culture. The minister's words that " the tasks of
culture do not suffer " were endorsed with genuine
approval at the most by the East-Elbean Junkers
who make limited demands on culture. These words only
caused the other representatives of capitalist society
to smile ironically. It suffices to put side by side the
German military expenditure of $1\frac{1}{3}$ milliards (£66,000,000)
for 1906 and the 171 millions £8,550,000) which Prussia
expended on education of every type in 1906 ; the 420
millions (£21,000,000) which Austria-Hungary expended
for military purposes in 1900 and the $5\frac{1}{2}$ millions
(£275,000) expended on elementary schools. The latest
Prussian law concerning the maintenance of schools and
the petty way in which it regulates the question of
teachers' salaries, as well as Studt's notorious decree

against raising the teachers' salaries in the towns, speak volumes.

Germany would be rich enough to solve all the problems of culture ; and the more these problems were solved, the easier it would be for the country to bear their cost. But the barrier of militarism blocks the way. The way in which the military expenditure is met in Germany (and in France, too) is particularly revolting. Militarism is, one can almost say, the creator and maintainer of our oppressively unjust indirect system of taxation. The whole Imperial customs and taxation policy which tends to exploit the masses, that is to say, the needy section of our population—apart from serving Junkerdom, this class of parasites (the tender solicitude for whom again, to a very large extent, is called forth by militarist reasons), serves in the first place militarist aims. It is chiefly due to this policy that, for example, in 1906 the cost of living for the bulk of the people, in comparison with the average for the years 1900-1904, went up by 10 to 15 per cent. Again we have to thank militarism chiefly that our system of communications (whose extension and improvement should be in the best interest of a sensible capitalism if it were intelligently conscious of its own interests) does not, by a long way, answer the demands that traffic and the development of technique make upon it. Militarism employs the system of communications as a milch cow, for levying a special indirect tax upon the people. The story of the last Imperial finance bill introduced by Stengel would open the eyes even of the blindest. One can calculate to a penny that this bill was called forth by the necessity to fill up the 200 million hole which militarism had again knocked in the state treasury. And the system of taxation laws, which places a heavy burden on beer, tobacco, etc., consumed by the masses, and even on the traffic (the air which keeps up the vitality of capitalism) forms an excellent illustration of what has been said above.

There is no doubt that capitalism finds militarism a burden in many respects, but this burden clings as

tightly to its neck as the old man of the seas to that of
Sinbad the Sailor. Capitalism requires militarism just
as spies are required in times of war and hangmen and
torturers in times of peace. Capitalism may hate
militarism but cannot do without it ; in like manner the
cultured Christian abhors the sins committed against
the Gospels yet cannot live without sinning. Militarism
is the inherited sin of capitalism which admits of
amelioration here and there ; capitalism will be purged
of it only in the purgatory of Socialism.

THE ARMY AS A TOOL AGAINST THE PROLETARIAT IN THE ECONOMIC STRUGGLE.

PRELIMINARY REMARK.

We have seen in the foregoing how militarism has
become the axis around which our poilitcal, social and
economic life revolves more and more, how it is the
wire-puller which makes the figures of the capitalist
puppet show dance. We have seen what is the aim
that militarism serves, how it strives to attain this aim,
and how in the pursuit of it it is naturally obliged to
produce even the poison which will cause its death.
We have also discussed the state-upholding *role*—not
very successful though—played by militarism as a school
for forming men's opinions and knocking militarist ideas
into the heads of those in uniform as well as in civilian
clothes. But militarism is not content with this ; it
exerts even now, in times of peace, its state-upholding
influence in various directions. Militarism is practising
and preparing for the great day when it will have to
deliver its masterpiece (after having served long as an
apprentice and a journeyman), for the day when the
people, impudent and rebellious, will rise against their
masters, the day of the great upheaval.

Its bodyguard would prefer to face this menace now and
not to-morrow, because it could with more certainty turn
it into a deluge which would submerge Social-Democracy ;
on this day it will massacre to its heart's content and

slay with bullet and shrapnel wholesale for King and Fatherland, with the aid of God ; it will adopt 22nd January, 1905, and the bloody week in May, 1871, as its ideal and model. Schoenfeldt, the commander of the Vienna corps, made the following vow to the bourgeois at a banquet in April, 1894 : " You may rest assured that you will find us, too, on your front when the existence of society and the enjoyment of hard-earned property are endangered. When the bourgeois is in the front line, the soldier hurries to his help ! "

Thus the mailed fist is always raised ready to strike a smashing blow. The hypocrites speak of " safeguard-ing law and order," of " protecting the freedom to work," but they mean : " safeguarding oppression," " protecting exploitation." If the proletariat displays undue liveliness or power militarism at once tries to frighten it back by rattling the sword. This omnipotent militarism is everywhere at the back of every action taken by our state power against the workers, and in the last resort supplies it with invincible force. This militarism, far from keeping in the background in readiness for great occasions, behind the vanguard of the police and the gendarmerie, is always ready to help even with the everyday work, fully conscious of its purport, in strengthening the pillars of the capitalist order. The cunning of capitalist militarism is char-acterized by the diversity of its activity.

SOLDIERS AS COMPETITORS OF FREE LABOURERS.

Militarism, as a functionary of capitalism, is well aware that its first and most sacred duty is to assist the capitalists in piling up profits. Thus it feels justified, even bound, officially or semi-officially to place soldiers, like beasts of burden, at the disposal of the employing class, especially of Junkerdom, to help it through times when there is a shortage of agricultural workers, brought about by inhuman exploitation and brutality.

The giving of leave to soldiers to gather in the harvest is a constant practice detrimental and antagonistic to the interests of Labour just like the orderly system. It also makes plain even to the goose step and parade drill monomaniacs the thoroughly unscrupulous and clumsy swindle of regarding the long term service as a purely military necessity ; it also calls forth anything but flattering reminiscences of the company system before Jena. We must remember, for instance, the much discussed decrees of the general command to the I.,* IV., X.,† and XVII. Prussian army corps in 1906. The numerous instances in which the post and the railways draw upon the soldiers for help in cases of increased traffic also belong to this category though their purport lies much deeper.

ARMY AND BLACK-LEGGING.

Militarism interferes directly with the aspirations of Labour towards emancipation by employing soldiers as strike-breakers under military command. Let us recall the case recently brought again to the fore of Lieutenant-General von Liebert, the present commander of the " Imperial Union to Oppose Slander by Social-Democracy," who as a plain colonel already in 1896 grasped the fact that a strike is a public calamity like a fire or a water-famine—a calamity, of course, for the employing class whose guardian angel and executor he considered himself to be.

The method which was applied in the Nuremberg strike of 1906 is especially notorious in Germany. By this method the men whose time was up were pushed into the ranks of the strike-breakers by a gentle pressure.

Three events which took place outside Germany are of far greater importance. (1) Black-legging by the military on a grand scale during the General Railway strike in Holland in January, 1903. The result of the

---

* The editor of the *Koenigsberger Volkszeitung* was condemned to a heavy fine in the autumn of 1906 because he was alleged to have libelled this corps by levelling criticism at the decree concerning the granting of leave during l arvest time.

† *Vide* also the reply of the general in command of this corps in *Vorwaerts* of 3rd November, 1906.

strike was that a legal enactment deprived the railway-men of the right to form Trade Unions.* (2) The general strike of the Hungarian railway workers in 1904. In this case the military administration went still further. Apart from employing the blackleg column composed of men on active service who, contrary to the law, were kept with the colours when their time was up, the military administration was not ashamed to call up the reservists and the *landwehr* men amongst the railwaymen and other reservists and *landwehr* men who were techni-cally suitable, and by brandishing the sword to force them to work as strike-breakers in the railway service. (3) And finally, the Bulgarian railway strike declared on 3rd January, 1907.—Of no less importance is the struggle which was inaugurated both by the ministers of agriculture and of war in Hungary at the beginning of December, 1906, against the right of the agricultural workers to form Trade Unions and to strike ; in this connection the careful training of soldiers to take part in blackleg columns for harvesting stands in the foreground.

In France, too, blacklegging by soldiers is well known.†

The fact that military education systematically fosters the willingness to blackleg, and that the workers who leave the active army become a danger to the fighting proletariat because of their readiness to stab their class comrades in the back, must also be counted amongst the international militarist acquisitions.‡

RIGHT OF THE SWORD AND THE RIFLE IN STRIKES. PRELIMINARY REMARK.

From times immemorial the military authorities everywhere are possessed of the capitalist truth of the words that behind the strike the hydra of the revolution

---

* The strike begun on 30th January, 1903, ended victoriously on 1st February, 1903. Already on 10th March the anti-strike law came before the Chamber ; on 6th April the general strike was declared, on 9th April the anti-strike law was voted upon, and on 13th April the general strike ended with a fiasco. The mills of capitalism grind with great speed when " Holland is in danger."

† *Vide* the " Manuel du Soldat," p. 9.

‡ *Vide* the " Manuel," p. 8.

raises its head. If at any time the fist, the sword and the revolver of the police have no immediate effect in so-called strike excesses the army is ready to cow the slaves in rebellion against the employers *with its slashing sword and its loaded rifle*. This applies to all capitalist countries and naturally on the largest possible scale to Russia which in its entirety is not quite capitalist and which, owing to its peculiar political and cultural conditions cannot be regarded as typical. And even if Italy and Austria march at the head of the column in this respect it is of great importance for the historical appreciation of the republican state form on the lines of capitalist political economy to point out again and again that apart from England the soldiers have nowhere been such willing tools in the hands of the employing class for crushing strikes and nowhere have the soldiers behaved in such a bloodthirsty and ruthless way as in the semi-republican and wholly republican states, such as Belgium and France ; in comparison with these Switzerland and America, the freest states in the world, can well hold their own. Russia, of course, in this respect, as in every other respect, cannot be beaten as regards cruelty. Barbarism, nay more than that, brutish ferocity represents the general cultural state of the ruling classes of Russia. Barbarism s the natural moving power of its militarism which, since the proletariat first started to stir in quite an innocent way, has literally shed in torrents the blood of peaceful workers who, desperate and in extreme want, were crying to be relieved. We cannot name any single event here, for that would mean tearing a separate link in an arbitrary and petty way out of a chain which is endless in time and space. For every drop of blood shed in all the other European countries put together in the struggle for economic freedom, a proletarian life has been taken by Tsarism to suppress the most modest aspirations of the labour movement.

The act vity of the colonial armies and of the detachments for defence against the natives in the colonies who do not allow themselves willingly to be pressed

into the yoke of the vilest exploitation is essentially
related to this method of applying military force. We
cannot, however, go into this question in more detail.

It is often impossible to draw a sharp line of
demarcation between the army proper and the
gendarmerie and the police. They work hand in hand,
mutually replace and supplement each other, and are
closely bound up together because of their very qualities
which here come into play, viz., the violence of their
attacks, their willingness and readiness to pounce upon
the people with blank weapons in a ruthless and ruffianly
manner. These qualities of the police and the *gendarmerie*
are, in their main features, a genuine product of the
barracks, a fruit of militarist pedagogy and training.

ITALY.

Ottavio Dinale published information in two instructive
articles* which go together about the massacres of
workers in Italy. He not only touches on the street
massacres proper, but also on those which had been
planned in connection with workers' demonstrations in
the economic struggle apart from strikes. The articles
show in a striking way how quickly the army in Italy
is upon the scene, what paltry reasons cause the military
to attack defenceless crowds with such extreme rigour,
how the military fire and shower blows upon a crowd
even after it has been broken up and is taking flight.
In summing up he shows that in Italy the "king's
bullets" smashed the bones of the Italian workers five,
six, and even ten times every year. He points out that
the Italian bourgeoisie, the originator of these massacres,
is the most reactionary and backward in the whole
world, that in its eyes Socialism is not a political conception, but only a kind of a criminal way of thinking,
of criminality, which is most dangerous to the public
order.

He quotes the words used by the Milan newspaper,

---

* *Mouvement Socialiste*, May-June, 1906, and August-September, 1906,
" Les massacres de classe en Italie."

Idea Liberale, on the morning following the massacre of Grammichele : " The dead and the wounded—these people have been overtaken by the fate they deserve—*shrapnel is the most precious element of civilization and order !* "

After such a standard has been set up one can feel no surprise that even a so-called democratic government like that of Giolitti never attempted to call the military to account for the bloody barbarities committed. On the contrary, the military were praised officially for having " done their duty." It seems still more natural that a motion about limiting the employment of the military in conflicts with the masses brought in by the Socialist fraction of the Chamber was voted down.

The shootings that took place in May, 1898, cleared up the situation in regard to the class struggle even for the blind and the shortsighted optimists. This is an almost complete record of blood-letting in recent years :

			Victims.	
			Dead.	Wounded.
Berra, ..	..	27th June, 1901,	2	10
Patugnano,	..	4th May, 1902,	1	7
Cassano,	..	5th Aug., 1902,	1	3
Candela,	..	8th Sept., 1902,	5	11
Giarratana,	..	13th Oct., 1902,	2	12
Piere, ..	..	21st May, 1903,	3	1
Galatina,	..	20th April, 1903,	2	1
Torre Annunziata,		31st Aug., 1903,	7	10
Cerignola,	..	17th May, 1904,	3	40
Buggera,	..	4th Sept., 1904,	3	10
Castelluzzo,	..	11th Sept., 1904,	1	12
Sestri Ponente,		15th Sept., 1904,	2	2
Foggia,	..	18th April, 1905,	7	20
St. Elpidio,	..	15th May, 1905,	4	2
Grammichele,	..	16th Aug., 1905,	18	20
Muro, ..	..	23rd March, 1906,	2	4
Scarano,	..	21st March, 1906,	1	9
Calinera,	..	30th April, 1906,	2	3
Turin, ..	..	4th April, 1906,	1	6
Cagliari,	..	12th May, 1906,	2	7

| | | | Victims | |
			Dead.	Wounded.
Nebida,	..	21st May, 1906,	1	.. 1
Sonneza,	..	21st May, 1906,	6	.. 6
Benventare,	..	24th May, 1906,	2	.. 2

Total—23 massacres claimed 78 dead and 218 wounded ! A good harvest !

In Italy there have been no end of cases (which did not end in bloodshed) in which the military were mobilized against strikers or against workers and " peasants " in general who had been compelled to hold demonstrations for economic causes. These army " exercises " on the other side of the Alps are part and parcel of everyday life.*

And right here we will mention what is commonly understood. According to Herve's† testimony it is just as difficult to count the massacres of workmen and peasants on strike in *Spain* (in whose dominions the sun at one time never set, but where at present it never seems to want to rise) as it is in Italy.

AUSTRIA-HUNGARY.

As is generally known, the state of affairs is not much better in the black and yellow dual Monarchy. The Socialist delegate Daszynski was quite justified in exclaiming in the Austrian parliament on 23rd September, 1903 : " In strikes, in demonstrations held by the people, as well as in cases when the feelings of nationalities are inflamed, it is always the army which turns the bayonet against the workers and the peasants." To show that the realm of politics was included here, he said : " We are living in a state in which, even in times of peace, the army is the only cement which binds such heterogenous elements together," and he alluded to the events in Graz in 1897 and to the bloodshed in Graslitz. We know that the military intervened and caused

---

* *Vide*, for instance, the *Temps Nouveaux*, 16th December, 1905 (Ancona, Taurisano).
† " Leur patrie," p. 99.

bloodshed in Vienna, Graz and Budapest when Badeni was overthrown in November, 1897. The frequent massacres of workers, especially in Galicia, are remembered by everyone (we will only mention that the blood of the agricultural workers was shed in Burowicki and in Ubinie (Kanimka) in 1902), likewise the bloody events of Falkenau, Nuerschan and Ostrau. For the latter, however, the *gendarmerie* is to blame—this special troop with its purely military discipline, designed to maintain order in the state, partly under the orders of the military authorities and partly under the orders of the civil administration. During the general strike at Trieste in 1902 there were also collisions with the army; 10 persons were killed, or wounded. The events connected with the masons' strike at Lemberg in 1902 also deserve mention. Political demonstrations in connection with the strike were held when hussars rode in amongst the crowd and fired, killing five persons. The riot at Innsbruck in 1905 which was of a purely nationalist character lies, however, beyond the scope of our work.

Excesses on a large scale committed by the military authorities against the people have frequently occurred in Hungary right up to the present time, and the *gendarmerie* naturally did its " duty " " thoroughly and completely " (*vide*, for instance, the disturbance on the Tamasie Puszta, when without any cause they shot at peaceful agricultural workers). One recent event should be borne in mind, namely, the battle which was fought in the Hunyad province on 2nd September, 1906, and in which the military wrought great havoc among the strikers of the Petroseny coal mine. Many persons were seriously wounded—two mortally—and 150 were slightly wounded.

The skirmishes and fights between the army and the proletariat, in addition to the political fights which took place in the Habsburg dual Monarchy, will be mentioned elsewhere.

In his speech already quoted Daszynski put forward the claim that " *bayonets should not mix up in politics.*"

But as everyone knows, they have, since that time, been made to take part in politics with ever greater force and determination.

BELGIUM.

In Belgium the massacre of workers is a long story. The events of 1867 and 1868 are important because of the intervention of the International alone. The ball was set rolling by the so-called hunger revolt of Marchienne in 1867, when unarmed processions of workers holding a demonstration were suddenly attacked and cut down by a company of soldiers. In March, 1868, there followed the massacre of Charleroi, and in 1869 the infamous massacres of Seraing and Vorinage.

The Charleroi massacre of miners who had been rendered desperate by the limitation of the output and by the docking of wages was planned and consummated by the military and by the *gendarmerie*. This gave the International an occasion to carry on a strong, vigorous agitation in Belgium. The General Council issued a proclamation which, in its turn, helped the International* to improve its organization in a signal way.

During the so-called hunger revolts of 1886, in which the demand for a general franchise, although not clearly stated, played a part along with economic questions, the scenes of the 'sixties were repeated. On 3rd April, 1886, General Baron Vandersmissen issued his notorious circular which was afterwards disapproved of by the Chamber itself. The circular stated cynically : *"L'usage des armes est fait sans aucune sommation,"* i.e., weapons are to be used without previous formal warning being given. The number of victims was uncommonly large : 16 workers were killed at Roux by one volley alone. And class justice put its stamp of approval upon all this by passing heavy sentences on many workers. From 1886-1902 scarcely a strike passed in Belgium without military intervention. About 80 persons were killed during these years alone. In the general strike of 1893

---

* *Vide* in this connection Jaeckh's " International," p. 69 and following.

the dead left upon the battlefield were numerous ; we mention this case although it was chiefly of a political character. The names of Verviers, Roux, La Louvière, Jemappes, Ostende, Borgerhout, Mons are burnt in letters of fire on the minds of the class-conscious workers of Belgium. They are blood-stained leaves in the stout book of sins of Belgian capitalism. The standing army was mobilized for the last time in 1902, during the general strike, when the reservists were called out. Unfavourable reports received by the ministry as to the soldiers' way of thinking and the mood they were in were soon confirmed by the soldiers who manifested their revolutionary ideas in a rather ostentatious way by singing the " Marseillaise," hissing the officers, etc. This gave rise to what had previously often been done, *i.e.*, the Flemish soldiers were sent to the districts inhabited by the Walloons, and *vice-versa ;* but it finally resulted in the standing army not being brought into use any more. Since 1902 the proletarian soldiers of Belgium have relinquished their honourable part of watch-dogs of capitalism, of being a " flying column on sentry duty before the safe of the employing class," in favour of the *gendarmerie* and the national guard, at least as far as militarism at home is concerned, as we have already shown. To protect its sacred privilege of exploitation the bourgeoisie at all events must itself move in the matter and risk its own skin if there can be any question of risk when unarmed masses are opposed to it. It has been shown elsewhere that the national guard performs admirably its function against the enemy at home.

FRANCE.

In France the history of the class struggle is written in letters of blood. We will not conjure up the hecatombs of the July battle of 1830 which lasted three days, the 10,000 killed in the street fighting of 23rd to 26th June, 1848, the executioner's work of Cavaignac, 1st December, 1851, of Napoleon the " Little," nor yet the sea of blood of those 28,000 heroes in which the French bourgeoisie,

D

the mandatory and the avenger of capitalism, howling with rage, tried to drown the Commune in the red week of May, 1871 ; not Père Lachaise and the *mur des féiérés*, the tragic signs of a heroism without comparison. These events—revolutionary in the highest degree—in which militarism did its gruesome work are beyond the scope of our historical investigation.

The heroic deeds of militarism directed against defence-less workers on strike began at an early date. The so-called " revolt " of the silk weavers at Lyons, whose banner bore the celebrated touching words, " *Vivre en travaillant ou mourir en combattant* " (to live working or die fighting) began in November, 1831, when the military fired on peaceful demonstrators. The indignant workers conquered the town in a two days' fight ; the national guard fraternized with them ; but the military soon entered the town without having had to draw the sword. Under the Empire Ricamari, St. Aubin and Decazeville are names made famous by their *debuts*. The bourgeois republicans fought hard at the time against soldiers being sent into the strike areas. But scarcely had these same republicans captured the political power than they began to practise the Bonapartist method they had just been fighting against and very soon even went one better. It was only in cases when a cleric or a monarchist was the guilty party that they found words of censure owing to political rancour. On 1st May, 1891, the new *regime* had its baptism of blood when a shot from a Lebel rifle pierced the body of Maria Blondeau, a young girl. There were ten killed and thirty-five wounded on the day when the 145th Line regiment was on duty. But the butcher of Fourmies Constant and his mate Captain Chapuis are not isolated cases. Fourmies was followed by Châlons in 1899, La Martinique in 1900, Longwy where the officers sealed the Franco-Russian alliance and celebrated it by the use of the knout, and finally, in May and June, 1905, Villefranche-sur-Saône* and, above all, Limoges with the cavalry attacks and the

---

* *Vide* in this connection the *Mouvement Socialiste*, 1st and 15th September, 1905,

fusillades of 17th April, 1905.* In December, 1905, the tragedy of Combrée† was enacted, and on 20th January, 1907, a mighty mass of the military was called out to keep off the streets of Paris those who wanted to demonstrate in favour of Sunday rest.

We must not forget to include Dunkirk, Creusot and Montceau-les-Mines where, according to the report of the " Confédération Générale du Travail " made to the international conference at Dublin, the soldiers declared their solidarity with the strikers.‡

What Meslier cried out at the recent great trial of anti-militarists is quite true : " Since the murder of little Maria Blondeau at Fourmies the working class in France has passed through a long martyrdom which claimed many victims." There is nought that could better reduce *ad absurdum* that illusion of the ancient " new method " of a peaceful development than precisely the fact that the great impetus given to anti-clerical and republican opinions and activity, so conspicuous in France during the last five years, the France of Millerandism, has produced no decrease but, on the contrary, an increase in the number of military " punitive expeditions " in strikes. Neither will any change be brought about by the recently established radical-democratic Clémenceau ministry with the two Socialists in it. Lafargue's caustic remark :§ " In so far as the modern armies are not engaged in stealing colonies they are exclusively employed to guard capitalist property," hits the nail on the head in regard to France, too.

UNITED STATES OF AMERICA.

It is easy to show how little importance is to be attached to the " tone of equal rights " to which the

---

* *Vide* detailed descriptions in the *Mouvement Socialiste*, Nos. 155 and 156, and in the *Vie Socialiste*, 1st year, Nos. 15-18. The National Congress at Châlons (October-November, 1905), after having rejected the motion of the Socialist fraction in the Chamber for a parliamentary inquiry, dealt a comprehensive resolution with Limoges and Konstantin's report attached to it.

† The *Temps Nouveau*, 16th December, 1905.

‡ A great sensation was caused a f years ago by the brochure, " L'arm e aux grèves " (" The Army during Strikes "), by Lieutenant Z.

§ *Humanite*, 9th October, 1906.

social and public life of the United States is attuned*
to show that capitalism knows how to keep up *its own*
" tone," and that very effectively, in cases of necessity
by means of the " *son du canon*," the crackling of rifles
and the slash of swords.   In this respect for the time
being, even in America, capitalism can beat the proletariat.   The following facts are highly instructive with
regard to the paramount importance of the military
method of recruiting and training of the troops, and
of transferring them to other districts with the view
of employing them against the " enemy at home."
The method of recruiting, training, and transferring
troops to other districts often bears a peculiar character
on account of the workers being frequently well armed ;
this arises out of the peculiar American conditions.

In America, as in Belgium, the period of the massacres
of workers begins with the unemployed movement.
On 13th January, 1874, in New York a strong troop of
police, without the least provocation, attacked a procession of the unemployed.   Hundreds of badly wounded
workers were left on the battlefield of Tompkin's Square.

Then follow the dramatic events of the railwaymen's
strikes in July, 1877.   The governor sent several
companies of the state militia against the strikers of
the Baltimore and Ohio Railway, but they were not
sufficiently strong.   The 250 men of the regulars sent
to their help by President Hayes were not more
successful.   In Maryland ten of the militiamen called
out were killed by rifle fire and a large number was
wounded.   In Pittsburg the local militia called out by
the sheriff refused to intervene.   The old trick of
transferring troops from another district was resorted
to.   Six hundred militiamen from Philadelphia engaged
the strikers in a short but violent battle ;   they
were beaten and fled on the following morning.   The
militiamen called out against the strikers at Reading,
Pennsylvania, were mostly workers who fraternized
with the strikers, shared their ammunition with them,

---

* *Vide* Lombart's " Warum gibt es in den Vereinigten Staaten keinen Sozia-
lismus ? " (" Why is there no Socialism in the United States ? "), p. 129.

and threatened to turn their weapons against any militiamen who should go against the strikers. But one company, which was recruited almost exclusively from among the possessing classes, and was led by a headstrong officer, opened fire on the crowd, killing thirteen and wounding twenty-two. The company did not enjoy long the fruits of its heroic act, but was pressed hard and soon had to beat a retreat. St. Louis which, for a time, was completely in the hands of the strikers, was finally won back to " law and order "* by the whole police force in conjunction with several companies of militia after they had laid a regular siege to the headquarters of the Executive Committee.

The horrors which swept over Chicago in May, 1886, can be laid at the door of the Pinkertons and the police. Mr. Cormick, manufacturer of sewing machines, let loose his 300 armed Pinkertons against the strikers— for the alleged protection of " those willing to work," and thus gave an impetus to the bloody attacks of the police, who struck out indiscriminately at men, women and children, killing six persons and wounding many. This happened on 3rd May. On 4th May the famous dynamite bomb was thrown, which was the signal for a fierce street fight ; in this fight four workers were killed and about fifty wounded, whilst the losses of the police were seven killed and sixty wounded. The gruesome judicial sequel of 4th May, 1886, which proved in a striking way what American democratic class justice is capable of is universally known.

The events of the years 1892-1894 deserve closer examination. First, there were the fierce fights between the armed Pinkertons enrolled by the employers and the strikers during the strike at the Carnegie Iron and Steel Works at Homestead in July, 1892. In these fights twelve were killed and twenty badly wounded. The Pinkertons were defeated, but finally government troops occupied the town and brought about the defeat of the strikers with the help of martial law. Almost

---

* *Vide* Hillquitt, " History of Socialism in the United States," p. 211, which has chiefly been used here in regard to North America.

simultaneously a miners' strike broke out at Cœur d'Alène (Idaho) ; in a fight between the strike-breakers and strikers, the militia, numbering over a hundred men, were not in a position to intervene against the strikers, who were well armed. Only the federal troops asked for by the governor succeeded in dispersing the strikers.

The switchmen came out on strike at Buffalo in August, 1892. The local militia which was called out at the beginning of the strike did not seem disposed to prevent picketing. Finally the sheriff was induced to ask the governor for troops ; within forty-eight hours nearly the whole state militia, outnumbering the strikers twenty times, came upon the scene and succeeded in restoring " peace."

During the same month the strikes at the iron mines of Inman, at the coal mines of Oliver Springs and at Coal Creek gave the State Governor occasion to concentrate the whole of the state militia, after several isolated detachments of militia had been disarmed and sent home by the strikers. In this case, too, class justice acted in a merciless fashion after the strike had been broken.

Finally, let us recall the Chicago Pullman strike of 1894, when the President of the United States, notwithstanding the protest of Altgeld, governor of Illinois,* sent *federal troops* into the state which, in conjunction with the state militia, broke the strike ; twelve persons were killed. It is certain that in this case, more than in all former cases, justice worked hand in hand with militarism and by means of the notorious injunctions and wholesale arrests helped so much to defeat the workers that it made Debbs, the strike leader, say : " We were not beaten by the railroads, nor by the army, but by the power wielded by the United States courts."†

Yet it remains true that, in spite of the fact that the militia frequently refused to act and that the strikers

---

* The same Altgeld who pardoned the Chicago Anarchists on 26th June, 1890.

† *Vide*, in connection with the above, Hillquitt, pp. 190, 209, and following, 286 and following, 306 and follo ing.

were often armed, military force was the decisive factor which brought about the defeat of the workers in all the cases quoted. During the subsequent period, too, the strikes in America " in the majority of cases were crushed with the help of the local police, the state militia or the federal troops," and undoubtedly also with the help of the " government by means of injunctions." According to Hillquitt*, who is inclined to be somewhat pessimistic in this respect, almost without exception the strikes ended in a defeat of the workers.

Canada.

Canada's free soil was stained with workers' blood at Hamilton on 24th November, 1906. In a collision with the railway workers on strike the militia wounded fifty persons, some of them badly.

Switzerland.

Switzerland's list of sins of this kind is truly long enough. As far back as the year 1869 the government of the Canton of Geneva sent the militia against workers on strike in addition to the police. In the same year the government of the Canton of Vaud recalled by telegraph a battalion which had started out on a march, provided it with live cartridges, and ordered it to march with fixed bayonets into the town in which the workers were on strike. In 1869 the government of the Canton of Basle in the same way made troops do picket duty when the silk weavers had struck to improve their pitiful condition. In the same year, when among the casemakers and engravers a strike broke out at La Chaux-de-Fonds, the new bourgeois government provided itself with arms and ammunition, anticipating that it might be necessary to mobilize the militia.

In 1875 it came to bloodshed. In the Canton of Uri the government (which, it is said, had 20,000 francs put at its disposal for this purpose by the contractors)

---

* P. 314, l.c.

mobilized the militia (at the Gotthard tunnel) against
2000 strikers who were trying chiefly to protect
themselves against the shameless truck system.   The
spirited attack claimed victims, and the battlefield in
the class war was strewn with several dead and about
fifteen wounded.   In 1901 blood was also shed in the
Canton of Vallais by two companies called out by the
government to crush the strike at the Simplon.   Several
workers were badly wounded in consequence.   In the
same year two companies were also put on picket duty
in Ticino to oppose masons on strike.   The well-known
events at Geneva took place in October, 1902.   The
workers of an American company of exploiters, who had
struck, were driven like sheep and beaten by order of
the government.   When at the time soldiers refused to
do police duty they were thrown into prison and deprived
of their civil rights.   We will only mention, in passing,
that members of the bourgeoisie who were not even
called out armed themselves on a large scale to oppose
the workers.   About the same time the militia was
mobilized at Basle to oppose a strike.   In 1904 the
master builders of La Chaux-de-Fonds asked the government for military aid in a strike of builders' workers.
To their dismay the strike was progressing in an orderly
manner in spite of all provocation and, therefore,
seemed hopeless from the employers' point of view.
The response was so quick that cavalry and a battalion
of infantry came upon the scene at once.   This tended
to intimidate the proletarians who were fighting in a
lawful manner, and they were driven back into the
slavery of factory life.   In 1904 there was a mobilization
of the military during a strike on the Ricken in the
Canton of St. Gall, for the alleged protection of the
fruit and vegetable crops which were in no danger
whatever.   In the same way St. Gall sent its militia to
Rorschach, where during a wages' dispute an excited
crowd had smashed a few window panes at a foundry
run by French employers.   What happened in Zurich
in the summer of 1906 was of a serious character.   In
consequence of the great rise in the price of the necessaries

of life several strikes had broken out which aimed at raising wages. Without any cause the militia intervened and caused bloodshed. They knocked about and beat the strikers in the most brutal manner. They dragged strikers, especially foreigners, to the barracks and there lashed them with riding whips. It was done at the officers' command, and this was not all : the system of picketting in strikes was forbidden as well as the holding of demonstrations of any kind. An interpellation in the Grand Council which referred to the disgraceful occurrences was first put off indefinitely and then strangled without a discussion by the compact body of the bourgeois parties. And to crown it all, six strike leaders were had up before the court. On 24th August, 1906, five of them were acquitted, but Sigg was condemned to eight months' imprisonment, and the loss of civil rights for one year for alleged incitement to mutiny by means of an anti-militarist leaflet addressed to the militia.

Indeed, this constitutes the limit of what one could expect of a bourgeois republic and of a militia.

A special light is thrown on these data by the fact already mentioned in a different connection, namely, that in 1899 the Swiss citizens not on active service were deprived of their ammunition. One can see it was done just in time to facilitate the employment of the militia in the interests of the employing class in the class struggle which was becoming more intense.

On 21st December, 1906, the National Council by sixty-five votes against fifty-five adopted an amendment to the Military Organization Law. According to the amendment when conflicts of an economic character " disturb or menace order at home," the mobilization of troops " thus necessitated " may only take place for the purpose of " *maintaining public order.*" The law was passed by 105 votes against 4. And without doubt the aforesaid amendment was neither more nor less than what had already constituted the criterion for the intervention of the military ; it is useless, absolutely useless, and the large minority which voted *against* the amendment gives rise to thought.

NORWAY.

Free Norway, which in the summer of 1905 passed through the most placid revolution in the world and crowned it by setting up a monarchy to satisfy a primitive desire, follows entirely in the footsteps of the capitalist states in spite of all the peasant romance which clings to the country. The employment of military force against strikers is no rare thing in this country of peasant democracy. An article in the *Tyvende Aarhundrede* of 1st May, 1903,* gives an account of this. We learn from it that in 1902 alone there were two such cases : in Dunderlands Dalen and in Tromsoe.

GERMANY.

There still remains Germany. It is just in Germany that the employment of the military in the economic fights is not customary. At least there are hardly any cases to record in which the army took an active part. The weavers' riots in 1847 were an exception, when the Prussian infantry killed eleven and wounded twenty-four of these miserable proletarians who had been almost tortured to death, and when class justice crowned the work by passing an enormous number of sentences of hard labour. Another exception was the miners' strike of 1889, when on 10th May the troops demanded by the " first president " von Hagemeister left three killed and four wounded in front of the Moltke mine, and two killed and five wounded on the battlefield in Bochum.† In the disturbances by the Berlin unemployed in February, 1892, the military did not intervene, but according to trustworthy sources the military of Berlin were held in readiness in the barracks on 18th January, 1894, in consequence of a mere rumour that the un-

---

* P. 53.
† On 19th May, 1899, the German Emperor said to a deputation which waited on him : " If I perceive that the movement betrays Social-Democratic tendencies, and if they begin to incite people to unlawful resistance, I shall intervene with relentless severity and shall make use of the power that I have—and that power is great." According to the *Freisinnige Zeitung* he said further : " If the least resistance to the authorities were shown he would have *them all shot down*."

employed had planned to hold a demonstration in front of the palace.

The cause of this militarist moderation does not lie in an especially kindly and upright way of thinking on the part of the authorities which take the decisions. Quite he contrary ! Germany has a strong force of police and of *gendarmerie*, excellently organized from the point of view of the employing class. It is not in vain that Gremany is a police state *kat' exochen*. The well-armed police and the well-armed *gendarmerie* perform here the functions which elsewhere are left to the military, and they do it unobtrusively and are more capable of adapting themselves to the many-sided needs of the moment than the military machine which acts in a more cumbersome and clumsy way. The number of bloody conflicts between strikers and police or *gendarmerie* is quite large enough in Germany. The tramway strike in Berlin in 1900 and the so-called Breslau riot in 1906 form no exceptions. Biewald's severed hand is only a particularly revolting mark of the raging and tearing charges made by the police, this product of militarism. Biewald's hand finds itself in good company with countless skulls cut open, ears, noses, fingers and other members cut off, and this good company keeps growing rapidly. The number of victims of armed state power in strikes would scarcely be smaller in Germany than in other states. It is quite impossible to form even an approximate estimate because the number of those wounded in conflicts with the police is not fully recorded or taken notice of. If in Germany there are fewer of these victims than elsewhere it is not due to the goodwill and humaneness of the employing class of the capitalist state. This is proved most clearly by the fact that it is almost a regular thing with us to assemble the military in barracks and to hold them in readiness in the case of big strikes. The most serious instance of this kind is furnished by the Ruhr miners' strike which lasted from 8th January to 10th February, 1905.* Such a result on the contrary, was due exclusively to the discretion,

* *Vide* also what took place in Landau-Kaisersla..tern in September, 1906.

moderation, stern self-control, training and enlightenment of the German workers. We need not entertain
the least doubt that the Prussian and the Saxon
governments would, with drum and trumpet, sword and
gun, take the side of the employing class in the economic
struggle without thinking twice, when occasion
demands it.

MILITARY SOCIETIES AND STRIKES.

As militarism strives to maintain militarist tendencies
in the men beyond their time of active service and to
spread them further through the medium of military
societies, it appears almost an understood thing that
military societies intervene in strikes. It is true they
are not in a position to display the activity of suppressing
the economic struggles of Labour by violence, yet they
may be characterized as organizations designed for
blacklegging. At any rate, in certain quarters they
would only too readily employ them in this capacity.
Only the circumstance that in spite of all precautionary
measures taken a considerable percentage of opposition,
even Social-Democratic, elements, is contained in them,
prevents the fullest use being made of these military
societies. That such a use is not made of them is also
due to the fact that in the conflicts between the employing
class and Labour it is just those workers who lack social
insight and are usually as mild as lambs who are the
first to become enraged and into whose heads is driven
an understanding of the class struggle and of their
class position. Further, excesses on the part of employers set up even the backs of the Christian and
the Liberal workmen's organizations. Nevertheless,
the discussion which took place concerning this point at
a conference of the delegates of the " Union of the
Military Societies of the Grand Duchy of Saxe-Weimar "
at Ostheim in June, 1906, is of great interest. This
discussion started in connection with a principle adopted
at a conference of the delegates. This principle makes
it the duty of every member of the society to get any

members expelled who prove to be adherents of parties antagonistic to the state, especially Social-Democrats. It turned out that participation in any strike or, at least, those strikes which go against one's duty of " loyalty to the Emperor, the Prince and the fatherland " was to be regarded as confirming the fact that a person holds revolutionary opinions inimical to the state. As it will depend on high personages who play first fiddle in military societies to declare where and when such loyalty is put in jeopardy by a strike, and as these gentlemen, like our police and our justice, are very prone to look upon every strike (which not infrequently hits directly or indirectly the interests they have most at heart) as Social-Democratic machinations, one can reckon upon productive work here being done by the military societies. But it will not be as beneficial to the employing class as to Social-Democracy, which likes nothing better than clumsy stupidity which only serves to enlighten the workers and to weaken the military societies. The military societies expel in a more and more systematic way not only Social-Democrats, but all members of trade unions which endorse the principles of the modern labour movement. There is no doubt that they thereby for the time being put certain difficulties in the way of trade unions in the smaller towns because the members, apart from the usual " pomp and panoply "* are bound to them by certain material advantages† often acquired by paying fairly high dues.

The military societies are strongly supported in their aims by class justice and administration which still have the absurd courage to treat them as non-political organizations though their political propagandist character oozes through every pore. It is a helping hand which these organs of the capitalist state are bound to hold out to militarism on account of their solidarity

---

* *Vide Sozialdemokratische Korrespondenz*, No. 21, of 8th December, 1906, concerning the " drunken brawls " of the military societies, named thus by Pastor César.

† *Vide* the appeal of the " Sharpshooters' and Riflemen's Military Society of Saxony " in the *Leipziger Volkszeitung* of 1st December, 1906.

with it and in the interest of their common higher aim—
the protection of the capitalist social order.

THE ARMY AS A TOOL AGAINST THE PROLETARIAT IN THE POLITICAL STRUGGLE, OR THE RIGHT OF THE CANNON.

As the political struggle is nothing more or less than
the class struggle in its most concentrated form, we may
expect to find in it direct and indirect military intervention. In the first place, militarism acts as an
economic power, as a producer and a consumer. The
ruthless exclusion of all Social-Democrats, or of those
suspected of being Social-Democrats, from the military
workshops, for instance from those at Spandau, the
unconditional surrender of the workers (who are subject
to the influence of militarism) to the reactionary parties,
especially to the " Imperial Union for Fighting Social-
Democracy," these black hundreds of Germany, at the
same time absolutely preventing the slightest contact
with Social-Democracy, show how splendidly militarism
has grasped its chief task—protection of the employers,
—and how it carries it out with military thoroughness
—in fact, it beats the Krupps and Stumms in its
eagerness to support and defend the powers that be.
For instance, the " Imperial Union against Social-
Democracy " rules in such a way in the military workshops at Spandau that it almost plays the *role* of a
vigilant who controls the thinking apparatus of every
worker of the king. Its word and will decide at once
what workmen are to be discharged. This has been
proved in a striking way by the events in connection
with the discharge of the executive committee of a
harmless union of unskilled workmen in the military
workshops in the summer of 1906.

A considerable influence which, it is true, is rapidly
declining, is being exerted by the military boycott which
is directed against all those publicans on whose premises
the working men's societies or any other bodies which
savour of Social-Democracy even in a very remote way

transact their business. This boycott kills two birds with one stone. It protects the soldiers from a possible contact with the revolutionary poison (this really belongs to the domain of militarist pedagogy discussed above). Further, it renders it difficult for the workers to secure rooms and halls for meetings, for often they cannot hire a single public room. In Berlin, for instance, it has turned out that the boycott cannot be made effective and has been almost abandoned, but our comrades in the smaller towns suffer* much from this " rat-plague " as it is, of course, directed against the economic struggle of the proletariat.

But these are " only its minor sins." Militarism is not satisfied with perpetually intervening in the petty everyday political struggles and with prying into them as is its wont ; it has infinitely greater ambitions. Militarism is the noblest and mightiest support of the throne and the altar in all the great and serious conflicts of capitalist reaction with the revolution. During all the former great revolutionary movements it likewise threw its whole weight into the scales. This need only be briefly indicated. We have already dealt with the gruesome laurel wreaths with which capitalist militarism crowned itself in the struggle with the Paris proletariat in July, 1830, in June, 1848, and in May, 1871, as well as on 2nd December, 1852, when " Napoleon the Little " provoked rioting. Of special interest here because they took place in England are the Chartist massacres of Newport and Birmingham in 1839 (in which ten were killed and fifty wounded) : " *Et tu, Brute !* " The whole of Russia has been under martial law of various degrees for the last two years to assist Tsarism in committing its cruel barbarities and to ruthlessly crush the liberation movement by means of the soldiers' fists, whips, swords, rifles and guns which are about to turn this unhappy country into a cemetery. Only the

---

* To this category also belongs the threat by the military to boycott (made during the Reichstag election of 1903) those publicans at Spandau on whose premises the Social-Democrats had displayed copies of electors' lists to facilitate the control of such lists. The publicans were forced to take down the lists displayed.—(*Vide* the *Reichstag Memorial*, No. 618, 1905-1907.)

advance of the revolutionary development as well as the disintegration of the army which, necessarily, goes hand in hand with the energy displayed by the revolutionary forces at the time are safe guarantees that this " Christian " but suicidal plan will not be carried out. As has been repeatedly remarked many reservations have to be made when Russia is considered in an examination of the capitalist states.

Significant is the part played by the standing army in the first great Belgian electoral fight as well as the *role* played in the second great Belgian electoral fight in 1902 by the national guard, this special militarist organization of the bourgeoisie for use in the class struggle.

Apart from mobilizing the military against the workers who held a demonstration in the Prater (Park) at Vienna on 1st May, 1896, and apart from the events in Prague, Vienna and Glatz (1897), in Lemberg and Triest (1902), Austria, above all, furnished a second brilliant example of militarist political action on a large scale in the electoral fight of 1905. As we know, Bohemia especially was on the point of becoming the scene of civil war.* On 5th and 28th November, 1905, the days on which electoral demonstrations were to be held, Prague (where the miners were out on strike at the same time) was crowded with and encircled by the military ; the surrounding heights were occupied by artillery ready to fire ; about eighty persons were killed, though, it is true, it was done by the police.

The events in Italy which belong to this category have already been mentioned.

We now come to Germany, that Germany whose supreme war-lord in a speech known all over the world (which has become one of the most effective weapons in the standing arsenal of anti-militarist propaganda in all countries) gave the soldiers a curious interpretation of the fourth commandment. The war-lord not only delivered the well-known speech against the " mob "

---

* *Vide* also the *Jugendlicher Arbeiter* of December, 1905 (regarding the shooting of the 16-year-old Johann Hubae).

at the Guards' banquet on Sedan day in 1895, but also made his famous appeal to his Alexandrians on 28th March, 1901. For the proletariat, the only sound pillar of the "constitution," were meant the military armaments and Wrangel's *coups de main*, with which in 1848-1849 the German revolution (betrayed by the bourgeoisie practically all along the line and left in the lurch) was shamelessly robbed of its birthright and crushed. Let us recall the chain affair of Boyen-Loetzen in September, 1870, and the bloody visions of Bismarck-Puttkamer memory. At the time of the infamous Socialist law these heroes of the 19th century anticipated and longed* to see the tormented workers forced out into the streets, cut to pieces by the military with the sword, and riddled with rifle and shrapnel in a thoroughly artistic and sportsmanlike manner. That the military were held in readiness in barracks in the case of May festivals† and Reichstag elections until quite recently is a fact only too well known.‡ The events of 1896 connected with the filching of the Saxon electoral rights and the partici-pation of the military in the "pacification" of the population of Saxony in 1905-1906 are equally well known.§ In the electoral demonstrations held in Hamburg on the "bloody Wednesday" in November, 1905, the police sword and revolver sufficed to do the work, while the military, consisting of natives of Ham-burg, were held in the background. It was due to the

* Ludwigshaven in the Palatinate was practically occupied by troops on the Sunday before the election of 1887, and only the presence of mind of the Social-Democrats prevented the rifles going off (*vide* the description in the "Memor ndum to the Party Conference at Mannheim," p. 9 and following, 1906). The German Emperor's statement recorded by the "Hohenlohe Memoirs" under the date of 19th December, 1889, is interesting in this connection : "When the Social-Demo-crats are in the majority on the Berlin town council they would plunder the citizens ; this would make no difference to him, he would have embrasures m de to the palace and would watch the plundering going on ; then the citizens would be forced to implore him to come to their assistance."
† This applied especially to the first May Day celebration (1890), which the military firebrands, the "military party" ("Hohenlohe's Memoirs," 14th Sep-tember, 1893), would have been only too pleased to have used as the occasion for a bloody settlement with the troublesome and hated Social-Democracy (*vide* the "Sorgescher Briefwechsel" ("The Sorge Correspondence"), pp. 384 and 387).
‡ *Vide* the electoral riots at Laurahuette and Zabrze in Upper Silesia in 1903.
§ *Vide* the order *re* firing for 21st January, 1906, published by the *Leipziger Volkszeitung* of 3rd April, 1906.

work of the police that two corpses adorned the pavement of the free Hansa town.

The 21st January, 1906, showed the defenders of Capitalism in their greatest glory. He who heard* the guns rattle along the paved streets of Berlin has, on this day, peered into the very heart and soul of militarism. This rattling of the guns still resounds in our ears to-day and spurs us on to wage our fight against militarism with unsparing relentlessness and a tireless determination.

On 21st January, 1906, it was only a question of a demonstration against the shameful Prussian three-class (electoral) system. But we know that our militarism would be just as prone to unsheath the sword and fire the bullet if it were a question of altering the state constitution in a reactionary sense by a *coup d'état*. And the latest Hohenlohe and Delbrueck revelations have shown how Bismarck, in 1890, was on the point of dispersing the Reichstag, filching its electoral rights, of driving the proletarian masses into the streets to face the guns and rifles, of smashing up Social-Democracy by shattering the defenceless ranks of the workers and of building† with terrorism and coercion a formidable stronghold of Bismarckian-Junker reaction on the graves of the shattered proletarian bodies. We have heard, further, that the German Emperor would not endorse this plan because he first wished to " satisfy the well-founded complaints of the workers and, at all events, to do all he could to meet their demands." We know that the workers hold an opinion entirely different from that of the ruling classes as to what demands of Labour are well founded. We know that the antagonistic attitude taken towards the Reichstag electoral rights, at all events, by very influential circles in the North of Germany is becoming more marked‡ (the most

---

* *Vide* also the Saxon order *re* firing (preceding footnote).
† As we know, the *Hamburger Nachrichten* brought this plan to light once more in March, 1892.
‡ *Vide* the Handbook for Social-Democratic Electors, 1903 ; Handbook for Landtag Electors, 1903 ; and, above all, the *Hamburger Nachrichten*, the *Kreuzzeitung*, the *Deutsche Tageszeitung*, and the *Post*, in connection with the dissolution of the Reichstag on 13th December, 1906, in case the result of the election should be unfavourable.

virulent antagonism to these rights was also shown by Miguel, the ex-communist, as the Hohenlohe Memoirs have revealed). We know that the danger of a " military solution " of the social question by means of rifles of small calibre and of cannons of large calibre seems to have drawn nearer than ever.* Should the chief of the General Staff, Helmut von Moltke, become the Imperial Chancellor, as has been recently announced, it would mean† to all appearances a victory for the notorious military court party.

There has never been a shortage of shrapnel princes, shrapnel Junkers and shrapnel generals in the history of the world. One must be prepared for everything. There is no time to lose.‡

MILITARY SOCIETIES IN THE POLITICAL STRUGGLE.

The military societies naturally manifest a very intense political activity which German justice, of course, cannot see as its eyes are blindfolded. Everybody knows how these societies are mobilized during elections and how they force their members to leave the opposition political organizations. Worthy of mention is the manner in which they show their " loyalty to the king " by depriving the class-conscious workers of their meeting

---

* The appeal to the Prussian bayonets made by the thoroughbred Junker von Oldenburg-Januschau in the Reichstag in May, 1905, and at the Provincial Conference of the " Union of Agrarians " in Konitz, echoed the heartfelt desires of, at all events, an influential camarilla.

† The *Berliner Tageblatt* thus characterizes this rising man : " Helmut von Moltke has the reputation of being a pronounced reactionary, tempered by a certain soldierly candour and a happy disposition ; it is even rumoured that he has spiritualist leanings. He is by no means a man of theory, but rather a man of aggressive action who is possessed of the " courage of sangfroid," and ready to engage in politics by shooting with the rifle and slashing with the sword." There we have the characteristics so eagerly wished for by our firebrands all centred in one man !

‡ That the element of satire should not be lacking in the tragedy, we will here refer to the farce which was enacted in the small town of Hildburghausen in Thuringia in 1904. The students of the Technical Institute were incensed at the police because they were not lenient enough to these young bourgeois who had a craving for causing disturbances. One night the students, who were in " over-buoyant spirits," stormed the police station, and could only be repulsed, though without bloodshed, by a company of infantry called out. The sequel to it before the county court of Meiningen also deserves to be recalled. The accused " rebels " were not—as happens in similar cases to workers—condemned to imprisonment or hard labour, but were either acquitted or lightly fined. But the unfortunate lieutenant who intervened, and who, perhaps, had not strictly adhered to all the formalities, was severely reprimanded,

places. There are only two fresh facts to bring forward :
(1) The decision of the " Society of Ex-Soldiers of the
XVI. Army Corps of Duisburg-Beek " taken in October,
1906, to boycott the Kaiserhof (Hotel) at Duisburg
because it had been hired for a miners' meeting, and
(2) the expulsion from the military societies* of Saxony
of those publicans who have halls to let and who allow
the workers to use their premises. It is no easy matter
to face these methods of fighting in the smaller towns ;
when the workers are well organized it simply means
blows in the air.

The material which belongs to this category deserves
to be systematically collected in order to be employed
in the petty fights.

MILITARISM, A MENACE TO PEACE,

Nationalist contradictions, the need for national
expansion owing to the increase in population, the need
for the annexation of territories which possess natural
wealth, to augment a nation's wealth (that is to say, the
wealth of the ruling classes), and for rendering the
state self-contained by turning it, as far as possible,
into a self-sufficing unit as regards production (a natural
tendency to extend the policy of protective tariffs, a
tendency whose signification, it is true, is bound to
grow less in face of the international division of labour
which is assuming ever larger dimensions) can even
to-day produce international political tension. The
need for facilitating communication within the country
and with foreign countries, contrasts in the general
cultural level, especially in the political stage of development, can also produce international political tension.
As has been shown already, the most important political
tension which to-day can implicate us in an international
war is caused by the competition of individual states
within the world economy, by the world trade, by the
world policy with all its complications, especially the

* To this relates the explanation given by the President of the " Union of
the Military Societies of Saxony " and inserted in the *Leipziger Volkszeitung*
of 1st December, 1906,

colonial policy. Those who are principally to blame for this tension are the powerful men interested in the expansion of industry and trade ; they may be designated as being interested in a *successful* war.

We must not shut our eyes to the fact that the existence of the standing armies in which militarism has entrenched itself in the *most striking manner* is a menace to international peace *per se,* an independent danger threatening war. And this quite apart from the fact that an increase in the military burdens, that " endless screw," may make one disposed to let no favourable moment slip by without making use of one's military superiority at a given moment, or starting a military conflict once it is deemed necessary in order to prevent a further unfavourable change in the relation of military power. As we know, this inclination did not fail to make its influence felt* in France in the Morocco conflict, though it rather determines the time during which a war breaks out than the outbreak itself. But the standing army produces, as does the militia on a much smaller scale, a modern caste of warriors, a caste of persons which, so to say, is trained to war from infancy, a privileged class of conquistadores who seek adventure and promotion in war. To this category belong also those strata which in case of war have an axe to grind, those who supply arms, munitions, battleships, horses, equipment, material for clothing, the means of transport and the commissariat ; in short, the army contractors who, of course, exist also in the states which have a militia, though to a smaller extent. Both these groups are " in the know " ; they occupy the highest posts in the state and exert a great influence on those powers which have to make a formal decision on war and peace. They miss no favourable opportunity of attempting to turn this influence (which they have first acquired by exploiting militarism) into yellow gold and to sacrifice hecatombs of proletarians on the altar of profit. As agitators in favour of colonies they drive

---

* *Vide* also the article by Major-General von Zeppelin in the *Kreuzzeitung* No. 600 (1906),

their " dear fatherland " into dangerous, costly adventures highly profitable to themselves ; and thereupon, as agitators in favour of a navy, save* the same fatherland in a different manner which is again highly profitable to them.

So that the fight against the standing armies and the Chauvinist militarist spirit means a fight against the danger to the peace of nations. The old saying : *si vis pacem, para bellum* (if you desire peace, prepare for war) might apply to some individual state surrounded by militarist states, but it in no way applies to the whole of the capitalist states against which Social-Democracy directs its propaganda internationally. And this saying still less implies the necessity to prepare for war by setting up a standing army ; on the contrary, *si vis bellum, para pacem*, or an inversion of the saying, applies to the standing army ; nothing is more likely to provoke war than such a method of safeguarding peace ! In the case of the aggressive economic and political Imperialism of our day the standing army is, indeed, an adequate form of preparation for war.

But true as it is that the peace of nations is in the interest of the international proletariat and, beyond that, in the cultural interest of mankind, it is as true that the fight against militarism (which taken all in all equals the sum total and essence of all the peace-disturbing tendencies of capitalism, which stir up dissension among nations ; in short, which seriously threatens a world-war) is a cultural fight which the proletariat is proud to wage, which it must wage in its own most vital interest, and to wage which no other class as such has an interest even remotely as great as the proletariat (a few well-meaning dreamers only prove the rule).

Militarism also disturbs *peace at home*, not only by brutalizing the people and by piling heavy economic burdens upon them, not only by the pressure exerted by means of taxes and duties, not only by the corruption which goes hand in hand with it (*vide* the Woermanns, Fischers, von Tippelskirchs, Podbielskis and Co.), not

* *Vide* the *Rheinisch-Westfaelische Zeitung* of 5th December, 1906.

only by splitting up the people into two castes though they already suffer enough from class division, not only by military ill-treatment and military justice, but especially by being a powerfully effective brake on every kind of progress. For the man who looks upon the further development of the human race as necessary, the existence of militarism is the biggest obstacle to such a development being peaceful and steady, for him militarism untamed is tantamount to the necessity for the existence of a blood-red twilight for the idols of Capitalism.

DIFFICULTIES OF A PROLETARIAN REVOLUTION.

So that the abolition of militarism or rendering it as weak as possible is a question of life for the political fight for emancipation. Militarism debases the form and the methods of this fight to a certain extent and, therefore, influences it in a decisive way. It becomes a more and more vital question as the superiority of the army over the unarmed people, over the proletariat, becomes greater in consequence of highly developed technique and strategy, in consequence of the enormous size of the armies, in consequence of the unfavourable separation of the classes as regards locality, and in consequence of the relation of economic power between the proletariat and the bourgeoisie, which relation is especially unfavourable to the former. For these reasons alone every coming proletarian revolution will be far more difficult to accomplish than any of the past revolutions. It is important always to bear in mind that in a bourgeois revolution the revolutionary bourgeoisie, which was the driving force, had been at the helm as regards economic power long before the revolution in the narrow sense broke out. It is important to bear in mind that there was a large class which was economically subject to the bourgeoisie and was under its political influence ; the bourgeoisie used it as a catspaw to pluck the chestnuts from the fire. It is important to bear in mind that the bourgeoisie had first, to a certain extent, purchased the old rubbish of feudalism, before it smashed it up and threw it on the scrap heap, whereas the proletarians will have to conquer that which was gained by the bourgeoisie with the help of wealth by going hungry and by exposing their own naked bodies.

PART II.

ANTI-MILITARISM.

CHAPTER I.

ANTI-MILITARISM OF THE OLD AND THE NEW INTERNATIONAL.

"THE Communist Manifesto," the most prophetic work in the literature of the world, does not deal specifically with militarism or adequately with its accessory significance. To be sure, it speaks of the revolts "caused in some places by the proletarian struggle," and thus indicates in substance the *role* played by capitalist militarism in the proletariat's struggle for liberation. It discusses in more detail the question of international armed conflicts, or rather conflicts between states, and the capitalist policy of expansion (inclusive of colonial policy). The latter is regarded as a necessary consequence of capitalist development ; it is predicted that the isolated condition of nations and nationalist contrasts would tend to disappear more and more *even under the domination of the bourgeoisie*, and that the domination of the proletariat would reduce them still more. One could almost say that the programme of the first measures to be taken under the dictatorship of the proletariat contains nothing laid down with special reference to militarism : the conquest of political power which here is supposed to have already been brought about embraces the " conquest," that is to say, the overthrow of militarism.

Special utterances about militarism begin to be made at the congresses of the International. These utterances, however, refer exclusively to "militarism against the enemy abroad," to the attitude taken up towards war. On the agenda of the Lausanne Congress in 1867 there was the following item : " The Peace Congress in Geneva in 1868." It was decided to work together with the Peace Congress on the supposition which was either naive or ironical, that this Congress would adopt the programme of the International. War was designated as a consequence of the class struggle.

At the third Congress of the International which was held at Brussels in 1868 a resolution, moved by Longuet in the name of a commission, was adopted unanimously. In this resolution the lack of economic balance is indicated as the chief and lasting cause of war, and it is emphasized that a change can be wrought only by reforming society. The power to lessen the number of wars by means of agitating and by enlightening the nations is ascribed to the labour organizations, and it is laid down as a duty to work indefatigably with this end in view. In case of war a general strike is advised and the Congress expresses its conviction that the international solidarity of the workers of all countries is strong enough to guarantee their help against war in this war of nations.

Now we come to the " new International."

The resolution of the Paris Congress in 1899, which deals with the matter, is of the greatest interest. It deals with the standing armies which it stamps as a " negation of democratic and republican *regime*," as the " military expression of the monarchic or oligarchic-capitalist *regime*," as a " tool for reactionary *coups d'état* and social oppression." The resolution character-izes the offensive policy of the armed nations as the cause and consequence of the system of offensive wars, and of the ever present menace of international conflicts. The resolution repudiates both the offensive policy and the armies, from the military-technical point of view, because of their immediate disorganizing and de-moralizing properties inimical to all progress of culture, and, finally, because of the unbearable material burdens which the armies impose on the nations. The resolution demands the abolition of the standing armies and the introduction of a universal citizen army, while it looks upon war itself as an inevitable consequence of capitalism.

This resolution as regards characterizing militarism exhausts the subject more than any other drafted before that date.

The proceedings at the Brussels Congress in 1891 were significant. Here the question of war, of international militarism was exclusively debated. The Nieuwenhuis resolution which designated war as a result of the international will of capitalism and as a means of breaking the back of the revolutionary movement, and which enjoined the Socialists of all countries to reply to every war with a general strike, was voted down. The Vaillant-Liebknecht resolution which regards militarism as a necessary consequence of capitalism and the peace of nations as an aim to be attained exclusively through the establishment of an international Socialist system of society was adopted. The resolution calls upon the workers to protest, by tireless agitation against the barbarity of war and against alliances which promote it, and to accelerate the triumph of Socialism by perfecting the international organizations of the proletariat : this method of fighting was proclaimed to be the only one to ward off the catastrophe of a world-war.

The Zurich Congress in 1893 confirmed the Brussels resolution and named the following ways of fighting militarism : refusal to vote military credits, incessant protests against standing armies, tireless agitation in favour of disarmament, support given to all associations which strive after a world peace.

The London Congress in 1896 again discussed both sides of militarism. It indicated as the chief causes of war the economic contradictions into which the ruling classes of various countries have been forced* by the

---

* And not class contradictions ! This side of the question is specially raised here for the first time.

capitalist mode of production. It regarded wars as
acts of the ruling classes in their own interest at the
expense of Labour; the struggle against military
oppression was looked upon as a duty of the working
class and as forming part of the struggle against
exploitation; the conquest of political power, in order
to abolish the capitalist mode of production and in order
to wrench* from the hands of the governments the means
of power of the capitalist class, the instruments for
upholding the existing order, was fixed as the objective.
According to the Congress, standing armies increased
the danger of war and assisted the brutal oppression of
Labour. The immediate demands again were : abolition
of the standing armies and the introduction of a citizen
army along with international courts of arbitration and
the people deciding on war and peace. The resolution
concluded that Labour could, however, attain its aim
also in this respect only after it had secured a *decisive
influence on legislation* and had joined hands internationally to establish Socialism.

The Paris Congress of 1900 passed a comprehensive
resolution about the capitalist colonial policy of expansion
and the international possibilities of conflict which
capitalism bears in its womb ; it also condemned the
policy of national oppression, quoting a few especially
barbarous examples, and devoted especial attention to
the struggle against militarism. The resolution referred
to the decisions of 1889, 1891, 1896, pointed out the
international and national dangers of the imperialistic
world policy, called upon the proletariat to take up an
international struggle with redoubled energy against
militarism and the world policy, and proposed the
following practical means : international protest movements, refusal of all military, naval and colonial
expenditure, and " *the education and organization of the
young people with the object of fighting militarism.*"

A survey of these decisions shows a steady growth of

---

* The latter is not really the object of the conquest of political power, but
the essence of the conquest itself ; safeguarding through organisation what has
passed into the hands of the proletariat .s, of course, a task of the dictatorship
of the proletariat.

practical political insight with regard to militarism
against the enemy abroad, and an ever deeper and more
specialized recognition of the causes and dangers of
war as well as of the significance of " militarism against
the enemy at home." As regards the means for fighting
militarism, however, the idea of a general strike against
war entertained in 1868 was too far in advance of the
time ; likewise strikes by soldiers as a regular method
of fighting against war was rejected by all the later
congresses, and quite rightly, under the given circumstances. The recognized means of fighting, however,
make only slow progress. The refusal of military
expenditure recommended to the proletariat is the only
direct political manifestation of power against militarism,
which goes without saying but whose immediate effect
is insignificant. All other proposals move within the
domain of propaganda in favour of changes in the legal
position and in favour of future actions, that is to say—
as has been shown elsewhere—in the only domain which,
for the time being, is largely open to the proletariat ;
even the refusal of military credits, as a rule, will have
to be looked upon as a means of propaganda of this kind.
For the time being the chief difficulty, especially in
Germany, lies in determining the form and the method
of anti-militarist propaganda. That in the congress
decisions the form and the method have not been fixed
in more detail is due to the difference in the external
and internal situation in the various countries, and from
this point of view it may appear expedient, even
necessary. Yet we must not forget that the tendency
of the decisions is to lay greater and greater stress upon
anti-militarist propaganda and to specialize this propaganda. The Paris decision shows this in the plainest
possible manner. It reflects at the same time
the increased self-consciousness of the international
proletariat as well as the growing conviction that partial
successes over militarism against the enemy abroad and
at home must be scored already within the capitalist
social system by displaying the class-conscious power
of the proletariat.

In conclusion we must record the circular which the International Socialist Bureau sent out in November, 1905, at the instigation of the " French section of the International " in connection with the Morocco conflict. It makes no positive proposals in regard to actions against war, only demands what goes without saying and is most elementary, that the parties which are affiliated to the Bureau in case of war should at once put themselves in touch to devise and to vote upon means suited to avoid or prevent war.

CHAPTER II.

ANTI-MILITARISM ABROAD WITH SPECIAL REGARD TO THE YOUNG SOCIALIST ORGANIZATIONS.

IN countries outside Germany, which have a capitalist civilization there is generally a vigorous and often a very strong anti-militarist movement. This applies, above all, to Latin countries, such as Belgium, France and Italy, but it applies as much to Austria, Switzerland and the Scandinavian countries, though not until recent times and in consequence of essentially different conditions. It applies even to Holland, although Holland has only moderate beginnings of militarism.

BELGIUM.

Special anti-militarist propaganda was started in Belgium about 1866, when the military intervened on a large scale in strikes, as has been described above. After the soldiers had been reminded of their duty to their fellow workers by means of leaflets* two anti-militarist newspapers were founded : the *Conscrit* and the *Caserne* (the *Conscript* and the *Barracks*).† The *Conscrit* always appears in January (before the drawing of lots takes places in February) and the *Caserne* in September (before the recruits are called up on 1st October). They appear both in French and in Flemish (*De Loteling* and *De Kazerne*).‡ In 1896 the Party handed over the publication of both newspapers to the

---

* We have before us one of these leaflets issued by the Antwerp branch of the Socialist Labour Party in 1886. The leaflet goes straight to the point and calls upon the soldiers to refuse to obey the command to fire on the people.
† In regard to the ac ivity pursued by them *vide Le Procès de la Caserne* (The *Caserne* Trial), Volksdrukkerij, Ghent, 1905.
‡ The *Loteling* and *Kazerne* since 1887, the *Caserne* since 1893, the *Conscrit* since 1899.

95

" National Federation of the Young Guards "* established in 1894 ; but they remain under the control of
the Executive Committee of the Party to which the
" National Federation of the Young Guards " also sends
its delegates since 1896-97. The " Young Guards "
were founded in 1893-94 (though there were individual
" guards " in Brussels as early as the middle of the
'eighties) chiefly to render assistance at elections and to
carry on special anti-militarist propaganda. Since 1902
this has changed. The disappointment caused by the
failure of the second general strike impelled the workers
to go to work slowly and carefully and to cultivate more
sedulously the roots of organization and propaganda.
The aims of the Young Socialist organizations were
widened and the promotion of education was given the
first place. Education undoubtedly is the steadiest
method of anti-militarist propaganda, or rather the
method which prepares the ground for it. Tempting
though it may be, it is impossible to deal here with the
history of the Young Socialist organizations in Belgium,
which are very closely connected with anti-militarism.†

We will only permit ourselves a few words. The
anti-militarist *Avant-Garde*, the monthly organ of the
Students and Young Guards, appears in Brussels since
1896. Since 1900 the *Antimilitariste*, the monthly
organ of the National Federation of the Young Guards,‡
appears also in Brussels. Since 1903 the National
Federation of Young Guards has published the illustrated
monthly, *La jeunesse Socialiste* (Socialist Youth), whose
place will be taken in 1907 by the monthly magazine,
La jeunesse c'est l'Avenir§ (To Youth—the Future)||,

* The Flemish organs were placed in the hands of the Flemish Federation
of the S *dlisttsche Jonge Wachten* in Ghent.
† *Vide* Houslaux, the *Neue Zeit*, 23rd April, 1904, p. 110 and following,
and the scattered Congress reports. There are three provincial Federations in
existence : the Flemish (about 1000 members), the Brabant (about 500 members),
and the Walloon (about 8000 members) ; the latter was founded in September,
1905. In 1905 the Liege conference dissolved the national council, which was
reconstructed in a somewhat different form in 1906 (the Flemish and Walloon
Federation elect each a representative ; the National Congress elects the third—
the National Secretary).
‡ The *Etoile Socialiste* need not be considered here.
§ Its forerunner was the journal *Contre le militarisme, pour le socialisme*
(" Against Militarism, for Socialism ").
|| It contained 16 pages !

now under the control of the Walloon Federation of Hainaut and Namur ; *La jeunesse c'est l'Avenir* appears at Charleroi since 1906. Both monthlies have been and still are full of anti-militarist propaganda matter. The same can be said of the Flemish *Zaaier* (the *Sower*), an illustrated monthly, published since 1903 on behalf of the Antwerp National Federation of the *Jonge Wacht* (" Young Guards "). Since 1906 it has become amalgamated with the general Party paper *De Waarheid* (published at Ghent since 1902), but it constitutes a special part of this journal with the sub-title *De Zaaier*. *De Waarheid* has a circulation of 3000, *La jeunesse c'est l'Avenir* of 5000.

Some local organizations of the Young Guards, especially the *Jonge Wachten* of Antwerp and Ghent, display a vigorous literary and special anti-militarist activity. The Antwerp organization, for instance, published the paper *De Bloedwet* (*The Blood-Law*) in 1900 for the purpose of agitation among the men called to the colours (its aim is the same as that of the *Caserne*) ; it also published the bi-monthly *Ontwapening* (*Disarmament*) since 1st May, 1905, and, finally, since 1905 *De Vrijheid* (*Freedom*). All of them spread anti-militarist enlightenment with zeal and aptitude. In addition hectographed bulletins are produced. Of course, the Young Guards do strenuous work with leaflets and posters, mostly illustrated.* They are now addressed to the proletarian youth, now specially to conscripts and soldiers. They have also an extensive literature in the shape of pamphlets. Cheap postcards mostly illustrated and of an anti-militarist character are sold in large quantities.

More than half the young men capable of bearing arms escape service in Belgium through the system of drawing lots. About 13,000 men are called up each year. Generally about 60,000 copies of the *Conscrit* and the *Caserne* are published at a time both in Flemish and

---

* During the drawing of lots in 1906 the streets were placarded with about 20,000 posters and 80,000 illustrated posters were disposed of.

E

Walloon together.* As a rule, they are posted specially to each recruit; the addresses of the recruits can be easily obtained; the recruits who have thus been singled out are waited upon by propagandists.

In January and September meetings of recruits take place regularly; also fêtes, processions and demonstrations of all kinds are arranged for them.

Contact with the proletarians who have been called up is not lost. In some (branches of the) "Guards" a system of rendering aid to those called up has been established: an allowance is made to the members of the "Jeunes Gardes" who have been called up, during the time of their service. The allowance varies in accordance with the length of time during which a member has belonged to the "Guards" and with the amount subscribed by him. In return the member is bound to furnish regular reports as to his chief experiences in barracks. The conscripted members also remain in personal touch with the "Guards." If a member does not serve in the locality where his own particular organization is, he is brought into contact with the organization in the locality where his garrison is stationed. It is obvious why we cannot go into more detail here.

The agitation carried on in the barracks plays an important part in Belgium. There are at present about fifteen soldiers' organizations (Soldiers' Unions) in existence which work hand in hand. Of course an effort is made to smother the menacing conflagration by every means. But though the organizations were often suppressed they always sprang up again, for their strong healthy roots lie too deep to be pulled up. At times two-thirds of the men in one regiment have been organized. Some of the Unions are closely connected with the Social-Democratic Party.

Propaganda literature is got into the barracks in large quantities, and is also distributed amongst the soldiers in the streets and in places frequented by the public.

---

* In 1906 an edition of 68,000 copies of the *Conscrit* was printed, about 30,000 copies of *Loteling*, a somewhat smaller number of copies of the *Caserne*. 100,000 copies of the *Caserne* were distributed for special reasons.

Soldiers' meetings take place. Numerous anti-militarist soldiers' songs have been widely circulated.

Of course, the Party it elf carries on a strenuous anti-militarist agitation. And the women and girls take an active part, especially in seconding the Young Guards in their agitation in the barracks ; their efforts are successful.

The pamphlet, *Le catechisme du Conscrit* (The Conscript's Catechism), which appeared in several editions in 1896 should also be mentioned ; it bears resemblance to the *Manuel du Soldat* of France and, like the latter, has been subjected to a fierce persecution by the criminal courts.

Anti-militarist propagandists are being fiercely persecuted. In 1886 Anseele was condemned to six months' imprisonment for an appeal " To Mothers " published in the *Vooruit*. This appeal called upon mothers to bring up their sons in such a manner that they would not shoot at the people. The *Conscrit* and the *Caserne* are continuously being brought before the courts ; since they first came into existence heavy sentences have been passed in connection with them every year ; naturally the same thing has happened since the " Jeunes Gardes " have published these two organs. The first case against the *Conscrit* was tried in 1897, when two comrades were condemned to six months' imprisonment. In 1904 Coenen, secretary of the National Federation of Young Guards, had to appear, together with five others, before the jury at Brabant in connection with posters which made an appeal to the recruits. The same thing soon happened to Coenen alone in consequence of an article in the *Caserne ;* he was, however, acquitted.* The sentences passed upon Troclet on account of the *Catechisme du Conscrit* in the middle of the 'nineties are worthy of special mention.

The chief crimes for which penalties are imposed are : Calling upon people to refuse to obey, insulting the army (six months' imprisonment is the minimum punishment !)

---

* *Vide* the *Procès de la Caserne.*

and lastly, the notorious " *atteinte à la force obligatoire* " (attack upon the (principle that) the authority of the laws is binding) ; in the case of more than five people conspiring together the punishment is doubled. Each year sentences of imprisonment which, on an average, total twenty-four to thirty-six months are passed. In 1903 the Secretary of the National Federation was sentenced to three years' imprisonment. To be sure, half the number of the accused was acquitted. The system under which the prisoners serve their terms is harsh : on principle no distinction is made between political and non-political prisoners.

The treatment of soldier anti-militarists is cruel—if measured by the Belgian standard. Dissenters from militarism are threatened with two to five years' correctional imprisonment, and the correctional system is very harsh. For the slightest offence the barbarous medieval disciplinary punishment, the *cachot*, is inflicted : the prisoner is made to lie in irons, is kept on bread and water in a fireless cell. The cells are built over water, are damp, and in winter their effect is almost fatal. In addition ill-treatment of the worst kind inflicted by sergeants acting as prison warders is a rule of the day. This service is imposed on the sergeants, too, as a disciplinary punishment.

It has been described elsewhere to what extent anti-militarist propaganda has grown in Belgium in spite of fire and sword ; it can boast of having almost scored a complete victory. In the critical year 1902 the whole population took such a keen interest in the propaganda that the officers who wanted to stop the agitation carried on openly among the soldiers in the streets were often assaulted.

The " Groupes des anciens militaires "* must also be mentioned ; they were organized formerly as a National Federation, but are now flourishing as local organizations and are publishing a paper. Anti-militarist propaganda in the reserve and the *landwehr*, as well as agitation

---

* Groups of ex-soldiers.

against the bourgeois military societies, are their chief tasks.

A few words must be said as to the attitude taken by the Belgian Social-Democracy towards militarism from the point of view of tactics. There exists no unanimity as to the attitude to be taken towards war, above all what tactics are to be employed on the outbreak of war. Only three facts should be mentioned :

The Party Conference at Ghent in 1893 expressed its enthusiastic approval of a telegram from the *anciens soldats* (ex-soldiers) of Amsterdam, which expressed the hope that the Conference would endorse the calling of a military strike in case of war, as suggested by the Dutch Socialists. The Louvain Conference in 1899 had straightway endorsed De Winnes' proposal that propagating Socialism was the best means of fighting armaments and of bringing about a world peace. In 1905 the Socialist Federation of the Charleroi district resolved that to prevent war it was necessary :

(1) To render the mobilization of troops impossible by calling a general strike of railwaymen ;

(2) To organize a general strike at the coal mines so as to deprive the belligerent powers of the fuel which they would need for the navy and for the transport of troops ;

(3) To down tools in the docks, arsenals and factories for munitions of war.

The history of the " Young Guards " also throws an nteresting light on the subject. Among other things, their Conference in 1897 decided to induce the Socialist Parties of other countries to organize their young people on an international and anti-militarist basis so as to render war impossible. The discussions at the Brussels Conference in 1903 were also of importance. Two sharply opposed views were about equally represented. De Man vigorously defended one view by using Hervé's arguments and his proposals were : to declare a military strike (collective refusal to serve), a general strike, and to carry on a revolutionary agitation in case of war. The other view was supported by Troclet and Fischer, who endorsed straightway the resolutions of the international Congresses. The Troclet-Fischer resolution was passed by seventeen votes against fifteen, two abstaining from voting.* At the Ghent Conference in January, 1906, a strict departure from anarchist tactics was made and individual refusals to serve were repudiated. A motion brought forward by De Man indicates that to awaken the proletarian class-consciousness among the soldiers means snatching the means of power in the shape of the army from the ruling classes. Another motion of De Man's describes the army in its *role* of opposing the enemy at home. The soldiers were advised to behave themselves as well as possible in the interests of anti-militarist agitation. By this means the anarchistic slag was got rid of and all obscurity was brushed away.

FRANCE.

In France anti-militarist propaganda is of old date and very vigorous, but it is not so well organized as nor is its trend similar to that in Belgium. In 1894 the twelfth Congress of the Socialist Revolutionary Labour Party (P.O.S.R.) at Dijon adopted a noteworthy motion against militarism in both forms, in which the harm of militarism and its common danger to the proletariat were emphasized. The end of the resolution reads as follows : " In times of peace the standing army serves as a police troop and a shooting machine ; it drowns in blood the struggles of the miners and factory workers who fight for their rights. And in stupid rage the proletarian soldier pounces upon his brother on strike."

Along with Social-Democratic anti-militarism, Anarchist anti-militarism developed as well as anti-patriotic Socialist anti-militarism—a special French variety (which, it is true, left its impression later on Italy and even Switzerland).

Anarchist and semi-Anarchist anti-militarism was

---

* *Vide* the *Mouvement Socialiste* of 15th August, 1903, p. 594 and following, and the *Jeunesse Socialiste* of August, 1903, concerning the debate ; Vandervelde's resolute attitude turned the scales.

chiefly supported by the weekly *Les Temps Nouveaux*
(*Modern Times*) and its numerous publications, which
are often clever and for the most part look at things
from the proletarian point of view like the paper itself.
They contain valuable matter and are written not only
by men like Kropotkin, but also by syndicalists, especially P. Delesalle. To these must be added the
publications of the individualist *Libertaire*. The International Anti-militarist Federation which we shall
describe later was also brought into existence by French
Anarchists in 1902, and somewhat earlier the " *Ligue
internationale pour la defense du soldat* " (International
League for the Defence of the Soldier) with headquarters
in Paris. The leading intellects of this league—which
seems to have since dropped out of existence—were the
Anarchists Janvion, Malato, then the editor of the
radical paper *Aurore*, Georges Lhermitte, and Urbain
Gohier ; their programme aimed at the abolition of
standing armies, the abolition of military justice, and at
securing material improvements and guarantees for the
soldiers ; but their activity went far beyond this programme. The picture postcards, pamphlets and placards
often powerfully illustrated, published by the League
continuously repeat the watchword : " *A bas la Justice
Militaire !* " ("Down with military justice ! "), as well
as the war-cries : "Down with war ! " " Down with
militarism ! " " Long live the peace of nations ! " The
league probably never extended its influence beyond the
boundaries of France.

The agitation for individual and collective refusals of
military service and desertion forms a large part of this
propaganda, which, of course, is anything but uniform.
According to Kropotkin* the military strike to be started
in opposition to war is not to be merely passive, but is
to go hand in hand with the social revolution and the
defence of the revolution against the enemy abroad.
This is to refute the chief objection to Anti-patriotism,
or, as the *Temps Nouveaux* calls it, Anti-nationalism.

---

* *Temps Nouveaux*, 28th October, 1905.

It is well known that Emile Henry, the terrorist Anarchist, threw his notorious bomb at Carmaux in August, 1892, in order to prevent, by this warning, a repetition of the massacre at Fourmies the year before.* The anti-patriotic Socialist Anti-militarism which betrays all sorts of anarchistic traits† is supported, on the one hand, by the Federation of the Yonne‡ department (which is practically agricultural) within the united Socialist Labour Party, on the other hand by a strong current within the anti-parliamentary Trade Unions. It is quite logical that anti-patriotism takes a back seat in the case of the Trade Unions which are facing the struggle with " Militarism against the enemy at home," the most cruel and powerful enemy of workers on strike.

Since 1901 the *Jeunesses Socialistes* (Young Socialist organizations) of the Yonne publish (in accordance with a resolution passed in 1900) a paper called the *Pioupiou§ de l'Yonne.* It was to appear bi-annually, then quarterly, as is specially stated at the head of the first numbers : " For those called up to join their regiments." All the state-upholding elements were let loose to run down the *Pioupiou*, which was sent gratis to all the conscripts of the department. It rained legal prosecutions which, however, generally ended in acquittals,‖ although the demand to disobey if ordered to use armed force against strikers was put in the plainest possible way. The *Pioupiou*, still published by Moneret in 1905, was at any rate strongly influenced by Hervé, who, beside Yvetot, was and is the moving spirit and organiser of anti-patriotic anti-militarism. In Hervé's work, *Leur Patrie*, is a detailed and clever exposition and formulation of his ideas ; since the middle of December, 1906, he publishes in Paris a weekly

* *Vide* in this connection the pamphlet *Le Patriotisme* and the publications of the *Libertaire*, Paris.
† The *Temps Nouveaux* is very friendly towards it.
‡ *Leur Patrie*, p. 246. This explains the oft-repeated objection with which Hervé is met, that his support in the Yonne is to be explained by the peasants' old, deeply rooted dislike of military service.
§ *Pioupiou*—a popular term for "recruit," with a certain affectionate, familiar note in it.
‖ *Vide Le Pioupiou en cour d'Assises* (*The Pioupiou before the Jury*), 24th November, 1903. Auxerre, 1904.

paper, *La Guerre Sociale* (*The Class Struggle*), which
renders vigorous aid to anti-militarism. No matter how
a war may have started, he knows no other solution for
war than : " *plutot l'insurrection que la guerre* " (insurrection rather than war), and he attacks most fiercely*
the attitude of the German Social-Democratic leaders
towards the question of aggressive wars. He by no
means advocates individual refusals to serve. In his
case the struggle with the militarism at home is relegated
somewhat to the background. We shall deal elsewhere
with Hervéism, which carries on its struggle with a
tenacity and readiness for sacrifice worthy of recognition.

What occurred on 30th September, 1906, is characteristic of Hervé's propaganda On that day Hervé
and a number of his supporters were present at a fête
given by the Young Republicans of the third *arron-
dissement* and by the French Educational League at the
Trocadero in honour of those called to the colours.
They made a demonstration against the patriotic-
military festival, and came in collision with the police
and were arrested.

In the report laid before the Dublin Conference of
Trade Union secretaries in 1903 the Confédération
Générale du Travail gives a good summary of the
anti-patriotic anti-militarism of the Trade Unions
which, in a strong contrast to Hervéism, underrates in
a one-sided manner the significance of " militarism
against the enemy abroad.'

In this report the methods of anti-militarist educational
work are divided into :

(1) The work of solidarity :

    (*a*) " The soldier's penny " (*Sous du soldat*) ;

    (*b*) Hospitable reception and care of soldiers in
        the *bourses de travail* (Trade Union homes) ;

    (*c*) Solidarity with those comrades who shirk
        military service or who are victimized for
        rebelling against discipline.

---

* *Vide* as to Hervé's anti-parliamentarianism *La vie sociale*, 16, p. 97
and following. In the *Mouvement Socialiste*, 1st June, 1905, p. 152, Fages says
that the *campagne anti-patrioti,ue* is in reality a *campagne anti-capitaliste* (tne
anti-patriotic campaign is an anti-capitalist campaign).

(2) Propaganda work : public meetings, social even-
ings, "send-offs" to recruits, processions, posters,
manifestoes, pamphlets, leaflets, the annual special
number of the illustrated *Voix du peuple* (*Voice of the
People*), the organ of the French Trade Union federation,
published since 1900 and circulated in great numbers,
often sent by post to those liable to military service ;
lastly, the soldier's new handbook (*Nouveau Manuel du
Soldat*) which already in 1903 had been circulated in
100,000 copies, and which, as is known,—with the
approval of Millerand, the ex-Socialist !—led to the
vigorous intervention of the administration and of the
judicial authorities.

The *Nouveau Manuel du Soldat* was published in
accordance with the decision of the Trade Union
Congress at Algiers on 15th September, 1902, by the
Federation of the *bourses de travail ;* a second edition
appeared already in the same year, and in 1905 a third.
The handbook ends with an appeal to the conscripts to
desert or to carry on anti-militarist propaganda in the
barracks, and with an appeal to those on active service
not to fire on the "enemy at home," their brother
workers, even when ordered to do so.

The former organ of the Socialist Revolutionary
Labour Party, *La Lutte Sociale* (*The Class Struggle*)
should also be mentioned here. It was published by
Allemane and Hervé among others for the "*Union
federative du centre*," probably for the last time in 1904 ;
it was devoted to anti-militarist propaganda.

In 1905 the Socialists and Syndicalists together*
circulated that red poster which enjoined the soldiers
not to turn their weapons against the proletariat, and
if ordered to do so, to turn them rather against the
commanding officers than against their own class
comrades.

Finally, anti-militarist propaganda is the chief object
of the French *Young Socialist Organizations ;* until 1903
each of the three French parties had its own especial

---

* With the co-operation of the "Association Internationale Antimilitariste."

organization (*Jeunesse Socialiste*). Since 1902 the *Jeunesses Syndicalistes*, promoted by the revolutionary Trade Unions, came into existence. At present they are in a somewhat chaotic state.

The activity of the Young Socialist organization of the Yonne has been touched upon above. Since 1900 the *Conscrit* (still published in 1906) has appeared as the organ of the revolutionary Young Socialists ; the newspaper, *La feuille du Soldat* (*The Soldier's Page*), appears as organ of the " *Union federative des Jeunesses Socialistes du Parti Ouvrier* " (Federative Union of the Young Socialists of the Labour Party). Both appeal to the proletarians in the soldier's uniform to bear in mind their duty to their class comrades. *La feuille du Soldat* calls upon them openly to refuse to obey if ordered to turn their weapons against the workers and to take part in the general strike when proclaimed. The *Conscrit* rejects emphatically individual revolts as being useless.

At the Trade Union Congress in Amiens in October, 1906, Delesalle pointed out, and rightly, that the former Trade Union congresses had declared themselves in favour of anti-militarist and anti-patriotic propaganda, and he announced that such propaganda had been unanimously endorsed by the Committee. At the same Congress a resolution moved by Yvetot was adopted—opposed, to be sure, by a large majority—which advocated a more strenuous anti-militarist and anti-patriotic agitation. It was evident that the minority was not opposed to anti-militarism or to more vigorous anti-militarist propaganda, but was opposed solely to the stress laid on anti-patriotic propaganda. At the Conference of the United Socialist Party of France held at Limoges in November, 1906, the same thing was evident. Only a few votes were cast for Hervé's resolution put forward by the *Federation of the Yonne*, which, after formulating the anti-patriotic standpoint, appeals to the comrades to reply to every declaration of war, no matter by which side it be made, by a military strike and an insurrection. But the resolution moved

by Guesde, which emphasizes the organic capitalist
character of militarism, which looks upon a general
Social-Democratic propaganda as alone being feasible,
and demands for the time being the shortening of the
term of service, the refusal of military credits and the
introduction of a citizen army, was also voted down
although against a minority three times as large.   The
resolution of the Federation of the Seine moved by
Vaillant was adopted.   The resolution, after stating the
principle endorsed by the international congresses,
demands that preparation be made to act internationally
to prevent all war and makes it a duty to use every
kind of action, from parliamentary intervention and
public agitation and demonstration down to a general
strike and insurrection, in accordance with the needs
of the situation.   At the beginning of 1906 Vaillant, as
we know, published in the *Socialiste* his celebrated
proclamation on the occasion of the Morocco conflict,
which ended with the war-cry : " *Plutôt l'insurrection
que la guerre !* " (insurrection rather than war !).

No decision has been taken concerning militarism
against the enemy at home.   Meanwhile many other
manifestations render obvious the attitude taken up by
the French Social-Democracy.   The watchword is :
Appeal to the soldiers to refuse obedience when employed
against strikes, against the workers.   In the *Manuel
du Soldat* the following appeal is made to the soldiers :

> " If they try to turn you into murderers it is
> your duty to refuse to obey. If you are sent to
> oppose strikes you will not shoot ! "

The famous words, " *Vous ne tirerez pas !* " (" You
will not fire "), which Comrade Meslier also used in
court during the big trial of anti-militarists in December,
1905, are only an echo of the general war-cry of the
class-conscious workers of France, whether they call
themselves Syndicalists or Socialists.   The appeal
already mentioned which was issued jointly by Syndicalists and Socialists in 1905 to the troops called up
contains a solution of the question which is most drastic

and fearless. The appeal calls upon the soldiers not to use their weapons against the workers, but rather, if the order to fire on the strikers be given, to turn their rifles against the officers in command. When this appeal was discussed in the Chamber Sembat declared in the name of the Socialists : " I am asked what my opinion is regarding the advice to fire on officers. My answer is that I approve of this advice in the case of an officer giving the order to fire on strikers." And Lafargue has repeatedly endorsed this point of view in *L'Humanité* without beating about the bush.

The numerous trials of anti-militarists which, in France, until quite recently nearly always led to an acquittal helped propaganda in no small degree. After having been acquitted ten times Yvetot was eventually found guilty by a jury of the Lower Loire in 1904, in connection with an anti-militarist speech and fined one hundred francs. Later he became acquainted also with prison life. In 1905 two Anarchists were arrested in Aix. One of them was condemned to three months' imprisonment for an anti-militarist manifesto posted on the walls of Marseilles. Morel and Frimat also suffered imprisonment ; sentences of imprisonment were also passed* in Brest, Armentières and Limoges. In the spring of 1906 there were convictions in Toulon and Rheims. The special edition of the *Voix du Peuple* for recruits has been confiscated again and again ; in October, 1906, Vignaud, the editor, was arrested. But, above all, we should note the big anti-militarist trial in Paris in December, 1905, at which Hervé together with twenty-five others was condemned to terms of imprisonment totalling thirty-six years, and to fines amounting to 2500 francs ; these severe sentences, however, were not fully enforced.

Anti-militarist propaganda in France has a vast pamphlet literature at its disposal. Apart from the *Temps Nouveaux*, the *Librairie de Propagande Socialiste*, the *Société Nouvelle de Librairie et d'Édition* (Georges

---

* *Vide* the *Temps Nouveau*, No. 12, 1905. For the persecutions of Loquier and Lemaire at Epinal and Amiens *vide* ibid, No. 26, 1905.

Bellais), the *Librairie du Parti Socialiste* (S.F.I.O.), and the publishing house of Stock in Paris have rendered a signal service by the publication of such pamphlets.

The success achieved by anti-militarist propaganda in France is considerable. In this connection we must not put too high a value upon the fact that here and there an officer embraces anti-militarism openly and takes the consequences* with the greatest self-renunciation. Such individual acts are of small interest in connection with a purely proletarian class movement such as we have to consider anti-militarism to be in France (as opposed to Russia). Of greater importance is the fact that the number of soldiers who desert, refuse to serve or to obey and hold anti-militarist demonstrations is on the increase. In these cases sometimes very harsh,† sometimes amazingly light sentences are passed, viewed from the standpoint of conditions in Germany. Thus two marines were sentenced to fifteen and sixty days' imprisonment respectively by a court-martial at Cherbourg in October, 1906, because they had exclaimed in front of a patriotic monument : " Down with the army; down with the officers ; no army is wanted."

We will only select a few details. On 3rd May, 1905, sixty-one men of the 10th company of the 32nd infantry regiment simply left the barracks on account of bad food and ill-treatment and went to a neighbouring place. In September, 1906, the soldiers arranged a demonstration in connection with the suicide of a reservist at the Compiègne garrison, sang the " International " and abused the officers. At the beginning of August, 1906, the *Eclair* published a circular of Etienne, the minister of war, to the corps commanders. He brings to their notice the fact that when leaving the infantry school at Saint-Maixent‡ sergeants had expressed

---

* The case of Merrheim nevertheless deserves mention here : At a strike at Longwy he appealed direct to his unmounted *chasseurs* to use no violence against the strikers even should they provoke or inflict wounds on the soldiers.
† Especially in Algiers the death penalty is imposed for the slightest offence ! *Vide* also the Besançon affair in the *Humanité*, 11th December, 1906,
‡ Which is to be done away with.

anti-militarist ideas, and had said they remained in the army in order to win over adherents to their ideas. Above all, we must draw attention to numerous strikes at Dunkirk, Creusot, Longwy (Merrheim !), Montceau-les-Mines for instance, during which the soldiers who had been called upon to intervene declared their solidarity with the strikers. It is no wonder that the *Nouvelliste de Rouen* speaks of Social-Democracy with regard to the army as of a " very dangerous wound on the body of France which requires drastic treatment."*

According to our German conceptions it strikes us that Etienne, minister of war, used exceedingly moderate language in the above mentioned circular when speaking of the danger of anti-militarism and how to combat it, just as it cannot be denied that in France great latitude has often been accorded to anti-militarism with regard to the constitutional right of the free expression of opinions. The reports of anti-militarist trials are very instructive in this respect. We have not forgotten how, a few years ago, the Socialist Fournière was permitted to lecture on social politics at the polytechnic school for officers. And quite recently the lectures for officers at the college for social studies in Paris—at which Captain Demonge spoke against militarism without restraining himself and in the most revolutionary way—caused our strict and narrow-minded militarists to shudder. If we take in conjunction with this the impending limitation of the scope of military justice and of the " biribi," the government bill concerning the shortening of the term of service for the reserve and the *landwehr* (though rejected) as well as Picart's plan of democratizing the officers' corps by bringing about the *unité d'origine* (common origin) of officers and non-commissioned officers,† France might appear as an El Dorado of militarism. The attitude of Clemenceau

---

* *Vide* von Zepelin's article in the *Kreuzzeitung*, 23rd December, 1906.
† First of all they are striving after putting the military schools on a common basis. There is to be only one school for each branch of arms, to be attended both by officers and non-commissioned officers. Our reactionaries are naturally horror-struck at the idea. *Vide* the *Deutsche Tageszeitung*, 22nd December, 1906.

(the president of a ministry on which sit two " Socialists," once *amor et deliciæ* of all social optimists) towards anti-militarism shows, as before explained, that it is not a question of changing the character of militarism, but only of changing its form, due in the main to anti-clericalism.

ITALY.

The various sections of the Labour movement in Italy bear some resemblance to the movement in France. Here, too, along with the regular political party movement we find Anarchist offshoots and an anti-patriotic syndicalist movement which is anti-parliamentary and closely related to Anarchism. The anti-militarist movement also differs in accordance with this division. The movement in Italy is not of recent date, but it has only recently been systematically taken in hand by the Party. In the first place, we must mention the Young Socialist organizations and, above all, the " Federazione Nazionale Giovanile Socialista " with headquarters in Rome ; provincial federations are affiliated to this Federation*, which publishes the *Gioventu Socialista* (*Socialist Youth*), edited by Paolo Orano ; from the first the Federation has been active in the domain of anti-militarism, just like the " Young Guards " of Belgium.

The " Leghe delle futture conscritti " (League of Future Conscripts) was founded in 1905 as a special anti-militarist organization subsidiary to the National Federation with which it is closely connected. Both these organizations are recognized by the Party.

At a sitting of the Executive Committee of the Party at Rome in October, 1905, the following resolution moved by Ferri was passed, only one member voting against it :

" The Executive Committee protests against the police prosecutions of the Socialists and of their press in

---

* Five provincial organizations and 24 sections of Northern Italy, comprising 2500 members, were represented at the Milan Conference held in 1906.

connection with the recent anti-militarist demonstrations ; with satisfaction it places on record the enthusiasm with which the Young Socialist organizations have carried on the anti-militarist agitation sanctioned by the Party, and resolves that the whole Party, with the co-operation of the Executive Committee, is to take part in this agitation, not only to enlighten public opinion in regard to the fact that huge sums of state money are being squandered on the military administration, but, above all, to educate the recruits and soldiers to the end that they, without failing to do their duty to national defence—should refuse to participate in murdering the workers ; these murders, owing to their frequency and their infamy, are a blot on our country."

As for the rest, the Party conference at Rome revealed the whole working of the anti-militarist propaganda in Italy. Anti-militarism was a special item on the agenda. Of two motions the following was introduced by Bianchi, the Syndicalist : " The Ninth Conference of the Socialist Party approves, in the discussion on militarism, the activity and the forms of propaganda of the Young Socialist organizations of Italy." The other motion was introduced by Romualdi, editor of the *Avanti :* " The Party Conference endorses the anti-militarist traditions of the Party and—in view of the fact that the bourgeoisie refuses to recognize that the troops should observe a genuine neutrality in the struggle between the workers and capital—regards as necessary, for the prevention of the workers being murdered by the soldiers and of blacklegging by the latter, to start an agitation which aims at inducing the young workers to refrain from resorting to arms in such conflicts and from becoming strike-breakers. At the same time, the Party Conference considers it necessary to propagate amongst the workers the idea that they should refrain from doing violence to the troops in order to guard against the soldiers retaliating and in order to prove that a common bond of brotherhood unites the workers on strike and the soldiers."

Anti-patriotic as well as Anarchist anti-militarism

was represented in the discussion ; Social-Democratic anti-militarism in the narrow sense, however, preponderated, whilst anti-militarist agitation among soldiers was only opposed by a few by arguments similar to those used at the German Social-Democratic Party Conference at Bremen. The representatives of the Young Socialist organizations explained that their comrades went in for anti-militarist propaganda not in the Hervé sense, but so as to bring down the army expenditure and to awaken the sense of solidarity between soldiers and workers. Finally, on the motion by Ferri and Turati it was decided not to put the resolution to the vote, but to leave the question for the Party Executive to go into. What, meanwhile, is of especial importance is that Ferri's so-called " integralist " resolution which was adopted at the Conference by an overwhelming majority contains the following passage :

" The Party develops a practical activity whose object is : to intensify the anti-clerical and anti-monarchical propaganda in view of the present situation and of the growing clericalism of the government, *to intensify anti-militarist agitation which aims at educating the Italian youth in Socialism so as to neutralize the tendency of the ruling classes which want to employ the army as an instrument of coercion directed against the proletariat.*"

In Italy, too, anti-militarist agitation has rendered the army unreliable as a weapon to be used against the enemy at home ; there also class justice has not abstained from fighting both the civilian anti-militarists and those in the army, by means of numerous trials and severe punishments. What happened at Turin in 1905 is well known.

SWITZERLAND.

Hand in hand with the more frequent employment of soldiers in strikes, anti-militarism has grown apace in Switzerland.

At the Conference of the Swiss Social-Democratic Party at Olten in October, 1903, a resolution was drafted which takes up the customary attitude towards war and demands a military consitution which "plainly determines the rights and duties of the State and of the citizens," and declares that the employment of the military in strikes is not to be tolerated.

Dissatisfaction with this resolution led to the summoning of the Lucerne Party Conference in April, 1904, which put forward the following demands amongst others:

" Considerable reduction of the military expenditure, decision by the people regarding expenditure of over one million (francs), placing the soldier in a better military and economic position, abolition of military justice, prohibition to employ troops in strikes."

The Party Conference characterized it as the duty of the Party to use every means for the attainment of these ends without indicating more definitely by what means.

The intervention of the military in strikes at Chaux-de-Fonds and the Ricken called for greater activity and the adoption of a more definite war-cry. Heated meetings were held and the Federal Committee of the Trade Union Federation published a leaflet on 15th September, 1904, containing the sentences:

" But in any case our soldiers must be enjoined not to fire on their fellow workers, not to draw their weapons against them, not only to refuse obedience on such occasions, but to try by every means to prevent murder. Only in that case will they act in the spirit of our federal constitution : ' The soldier in uniform is in the first place a citizen.' "

The Party Conference held soon after at Zurich passed the following resolution :

" The Social-Democratic Party calls upon the soldiers, when they are mobilized in cases of strikes, to bear in mind their solidarity with the workers on strike and not to allow themselves to be employed in actions which would nullify the right of their class comrades to strike and to assemble."

The Party Conference at Geneva which followed instructed the Executive Committee to draft a resolution on the military question for the next Party Conference.

In the meantime anti-militarist agitation was organized and systematized. In 1905 a Swiss Anti-militarist League was established whose object is :

1. To enlighten the workers in regard to the fact that within bourgeois society the army acts as a hindrance to the liberation of the workers ;

2. To advocate any methods suitable to render harmless the army as a means of power for the capitalists.

The League held its first conference in October, 1905, and has grown quickly since then. It issues leaflets addressed to the workers' organizations and pamphlets addressed to agricultural and industrial workers, and displays great activity. Among the pamphlets special mention must be made of the widely circulated little work, "The Watchdog of Capitalism," which has become almost classical.

In accordance with the resolution of the Lucerne Conference held in January, 1906, preparations were made for a central library and for the translation of Hervé's *Leur Patrie* (" Their Fatherland "). In addition the League publishes the *Vorposten*, which devotes itself with great skill to anti-militarist agitation.* Towards the question of militarism against the enemy abroad the League takes up the attitude which has been so much criticized, namely : that although the victory of Socialism alone will do away with war, something must be done before this victory is gained to prevent the " mutual slaughter of the propertiless by the propertiless at the command of the possessing classes," and that the only thing that can be done in this case is the " withdrawal of the military labour power," *i.e.*, the military strike. With regard to the question of militarism against the enemy at home they naturally agree with the (appeal) : *Vous ne tirerez pas !* (" Don't shoot ! ").† Obviously the first proposal is far less

---

* The League has a very impressive song of its own, sung to the tune of " Heil Dir im Siegerkranz."

† *Vide* in the *Vorposten* " The Draft Resolutions of the Party Committee."

disagreeable to capitalism, especially in Switzerland, than the latter ; all the same it is in accordance with a favourite Machiavelian manœuvre of the bourgeoisie that it should try to work its mill of counter-agitation with "patriotic" wind ; and it endeavours to raise this wind by indignantly stamping this tendency as "being traitorous to one's country," which "eschews the fatherland" and "undermines national defence against the enemy abroad."

The Party Conference at Aarau in February, 1906, was the occasion for a very interesting anti-militarist debate. It came to light that in Switzerland, too, the idea of the military strike, of refusing military service against the enemy abroad in particular has its supporters. The following important resolution was passed :

"1. The Social-Democratic Party of Switzerland strives conjointly with the Social-Democratic Parties of other countries to abolish all possibilities of war and the instruments of war amongst civilized peoples. It demands that international conflicts be settled by courts of arbitration.

"2. As long as this state of things is not established among the peoples of Central Europe, the Party recognizes only a citizen army destined exclusively to protect the country from attacks from without.

"3. The Party protests against the employment of soldiers in strikes. Since in recent years soldiers have been thus, wrongly, employed the Party demands guarantees against a repetition of such a practice. As long as these guarantees are not forthcoming, the Party advises the soldiers to refuse obedience when ordered to attack strikers or to draw their weapons against them. The Social-Democratic Party will endeavour, as far as possible, to ease the financial position of the individual and his family who are hit and, for this purpose, will get into communication with the Trade Union organizations. The Party is of opinion that the best guarantee against the employment of troops in cases of strikes lies in the strengthening of its political power both in the commune and in the state.

" 4. The Party demands a military organization which is based upon general military service and which is in harmony with democratic institutions and not contrary to the principle of equal rights for all under the constitution. It demands that the military expenditure be reduced and opposes all expenditure which is not absolutely necessitated by national defence."

As a result of this resolution it was decided to establish a fund for supporting resisters.

Paragraphs 1, 2 and 4 of this decision practically cover the draft resolution submitted by the Executive Committee. The Party Conference, however, embodied paragraph 3 in the draft resolution of the Executive Committee—the passage which requests soldiers to disobey orders when intervening in strikes ; the Conference made the wording of this resolution considerably more incisive and more definite, in accordance with the demand made by the *Vorposten*.

As is known, the Social-Democrats of the *Gruetli* (Union) take up largely quite a perverse lower middle-class attitude towards militarism ; they, for instance, condemn the refusal to vote for the budget ! It is no wonder that when the military question is applied as a test they will be found so light in weight that they will again be blown out of the Party like chaff before the wind. The fresh Party split rumoured to take place at the Aarau Conference has been avoided so far in spite of the strong anti-militarist attitude taken up by the Conference.

The publications of the workers' study circle at St. Imier are also worthy of mention ; they include the useful pamphlet, "Army and Strikes." The Young Socialist organizations which probably exist only in the French part of Switzerland also play a certain part. The periodical, *La Jeunesse Socialiste*, has been published at Lausanne by several of these organizations since 1903 ; later, however, it lost the character of a Young Socialist paper. We should also mention the Young Fellows' Society, founded and conducted by Comrade Pflueger (Pastor) at Zurich.

It goes without saying that in Switzerland, too, Anarchism devotes its attention to anti-militarism. There is in Geneva an Anarchist anti-militarist group, apparently the only group in the whole of Switzerland affiliated to the International Anti-militarist Association of which we shall speak later. The Anarchist *Weckruf*, published at Zurich since 1902, looks upon anti-militarist agitation—in the Anarchist sense, of course—as one of its chief tasks. We must not overlook the fact that it is proletarian Anarchism which is being put forward here, or, rather, that the anti-militarist arguments advanced by the *Weckruf* are, to a great extent, proletarian. The success attained by the Swiss anti-militarism, as evidenced especially by the Geneva and Zurich strikes, has already been touched upon, likewise the subsequent memorable action taken by the courts of justice in connection therewith. In addition let us record the fact that many proletarian militiamen refused to march against the masons on strike at La Chaux-de-Fonds ; in spite of the alleged " sympathy " of so-called " public opinion," grave sentences* were passed on six of the militiamen.

AUSTRIA.

It is only since the special Young Socialist movement came into existence that we can speak of a special anti-militarist movement in Austria. The Young Socialist movement apparently started in Vienna at the beginning of 1894 when the Society of Young Assistant Workers was established, which directed its agitation against the national Young Men's Societies and the Catholic Youths' Societies, and was soon copied in other

---

* *Vide* also Leo Tolstoy's "To Soldiers and Young People" (Charlottenburg, 1905, pp. 15-16 (cases of individual refusal) ; further, the *Temps Nouveaux*, No. 26, 1905 (four months' imprisonment without deduction of the term of preliminary confinement, and the loss of civil rights for two years).

places. Since 15th October, 1902, the *Jugendlicher Arbeiter* (*The Youthful Worker*) was published, first bi-monthly, later monthly and in greater bulk, as the organ representing the interests of young workers in Germany (Austria ?). The Imperial Union of Young Workers in Austria embracing all the local societies, was founded at Easter in 1903. Since 1st April, 1903, the *Jugendlicher Arbeiter* is the official organ of the Imperial Union. A glance at the issues of this well-edited paper which have already appeared shows that it has understood how to wage skilfully its fight against militarism amongst the young people.

Further, we must draw attention to the popular pamphlet already mentioned, " The Soldier's Life is Merry," published in Vienna as early as 1896. It splendidly portrays the sins of militarism in their special Austrian colouring and exposes them mercilessly. We must also mention the collection *Lichtstrahlen* (" Rays of Light ") issued by the same publisher ; it includes the pamphlets, " 200 Millions for New Guns " and " The Murderous Militarism of Austria." To this category belongs also the wholesale distribution of Daszynski's speech in the Reichsrat on 25th September, 1903, under the title, " Down with Militarism and Dualism."

The Czech anti-militarism deserves special consideration. Here, too, the Young Socialist movement plays an important part. The paper for young people, *Sbornik Mladeze*, appears since 1st May, 1900. The Czech Young Socialist organizations have announced that anti-militarist agitation is one of their special tasks. It is true the Social-Democratic Party Conference at Budweis in 1900 refused to sanction the formation of special organizations of young workers. This, however, was aimed only at organizations outside the Party and led to the Young Socialist organizations becoming more closely united with the general Party movement. The systematic organization of the young people is making good progress. In many places propaganda committees were formed whose special task it was to carry on agitation among the young workers. Since 15th May,

1901, the *Sbornik Mladeze* appeared monthly; since 1st January, 1905, it appears bi-monthly. The Social-Democratic Party Conference held at Prague in 1902 pronounced in favour of carrying on a special agitation among the young people and of organizing them within the Party.

In 1903 a Union of Workers' athletic clubs was founded, which also concerns itself with the young people in particular. In Prague a permanent propaganda committee was founded in December, 1904; other towns followed suit.

On 29th April, at Prague, was held the first conference of the Czech Young Social-Democrats, at which 22 Young Socialist committees were represented by 127 delegates. Agitation was carried on at numerous private and public meetings. The *Sbornik Mladeze* devotes a special column to the discussion of militarism; this has frequently caused it to be confiscated. A workers' academy which is well attended was established at Prague. The conflicts of the nationalists with militarism (the language question and the violence done to individual soldiers) intensify the anti-militarist tendencies. Special mention should be given to the case of Nemrava, a soldier, who refused to bear arms and was punished in consequence. Processions of recruits in mourning seated on red waggons and accompanied by funeral music became a regular feature in the towns.

What occurred during the electoral fights of recent years has proved that the army can no longer be looked upon as a perfectly safe prop of the ruling classes and of reaction.

HUNGARY.

In Hungary where the Party and the Trade Unions are one and the same thing, or rather, where the Party exists only in the form of Trade Unions, a young people's movement was started at Budapest in 1894, in the form of unattached branches of apprentices' organizations under the guidance of adults. The prime object was education, but the movement broke down in 1897 in consequence of the terrible persecution of the Socialists by Banffy, the "saviour of the bourgeoisie." After Banffy's fall, in 1899, branches of the Workers' Education Associations were started for young workers, which also devoted themselves to the education of their members. They, too, succumbed in consequence of brutal persecution by the police and the courts of justice in the winter of 1901-1902. The young people were scattered and joined the general workers' educational and trade societies. The inrushing tide of the powerful economic boom of 1904, during which the number of organized Trade Union workers increased five-fold (rising from 8000 to 41,000 members), carried also the Young Socialists out of shallow waters. The movement, which is still steadily increasing, acquired also a socio-political character. The outward form was that of educational societies or of unaffiliated organizations (in the provinces), or in some places, as at Pressburg, for instance, of athletic clubs. In spite of all chicanery, brutal treatment, surprise attacks, convictions and confiscations, the organizations flourished. With the assistance of adult workers a paper, *Ifjú Munkás* (*The Youthful Worker*), was called into being ; it constitutes the corner stone of the movement which is being fostered everywhere by the Party ; its circulation is about 1500 copies at present. The "Young Workers' Union" was founded in April, 1906, and it is still—in December, 1906—awaiting in vain the ministerial sanction for which it applied. The organizations openly endorse Socialism. Unfortunately, it has not been possible to establish the fact whether they carry on special anti-militarist propaganda and in what form.

HOLLAND.

Apart from the great railway workers' strike of January, 1903, already discussed, militarism has not yet become very oppressive in Holland. In consequence the activity of the Dutch Young Socialist Union, " De Zaaier, Bond voor Jonge Arbeiders en Arbeidsters in Nederland,"* founded in 1900 (temporarily suspended in 1903 and reorganized in 1906) in regard to anti-militarism has been of secondary importance.

In its paper, *De Zaaier†* (published since 1906), which is admirably edited by Roland Holst, the struggle against militarism nevertheless takes up considerable space.

In the winter of 1902-1903, Holland's " red winter," numerous anti-militarist meetings were arranged by Comrade Roland Holst, especially in Amsterdam. At the " Zaaier " Congress held at Utrecht on 8th April, 1906, a resolution which characterized the class character of militarism was passed unanimously. The congress enjoined the " Union " to enlighten the young workers in regard to this character of militarism by means of meetings, courses of lectures, especially during the period of recruiting, by leaflets and manifestoes, and as far as possible always to act conjointly with the Social-Democratic Party when carrying on this propaganda. Meetings against militarism are held every year in October when the recruits are called up. A meeting was held by the " Zaaier " at Amsterdam at the beginning of October, 1906, at which, after a speech by Mendels, a clear line of demarcation was drawn in regard to Anarchist anti-militarism.

Both the Party congresses and the Trade Union congresses have occupied themselves much with the question of anti-militarism, especially with propaganda among the military.

The " Socialistische Jongelieden Bond " has long existed in Holland ; it publishes, or used to publish, the paper *De Jonge Werker*, edited by Wink, the Communist Anarchist ; the " Bond " is under the guiding influence of Anarchists, but does not openly endorse Anarchism. Its membership is very small ; it appears

---

* " The Sower. Union of Young Working Men and Women of the Netherlands."
† The Party Committee, however, refused to support it owing to formal reasons. Prior to this the " Bond " for a long time subscribed to the Belgian-Flemish *Zaaier* as its official organ.

to be in a chronic state of undergoing re-organization. There is, of course, the typically Anarchist anti-militarism, prominent on account of the personality of Nieuwenhuis.

There exists, further, a " Bond van Miliciens en Oud-Miliciens " which publishes since 1903 the monthly *De Milicien*, edited by the Socialist deputy Ter Laan. This League is a kind of politically neutral trade society with a programme which aims at eradicating military abuses. Its counterpart is the naval men's union, the " Matrozenbond," whose organ *Het Anker* is edited by Comrade Meyer and published at Helder. It has done much good in the way of improving the position of the men in the navy, and has also planned and set strike movements going. At times a strong onslaught has been made upon it by the state authorities, which dealt summarily with the leaders and prohibited the sale of the *Anker* on board ship. The Chamber has often been occupied with this " Bond."

SWEDEN.

The Social-Democratic Young People's Movement made its appearance in Sweden in the middle of the 'nineties. The Young Socialist clubs amalgamated and formed the Young Socialist Union, the *Brand* being the organ of the " Union," which had its headquarters at Landskrona. The Union was not looked upon favourably by the Party and it gradually ran into an Anarchistic channel, as was rendered especially apparent by its attitude towards national defence and militarism against the enemy abroad. In opposition to this Union the excellently organized Social-Democratic Young People's Union was formed at Malmoe in 1903 ; since 1st January, 1906, it publishes the *Fram* (*Forward*), a weighty monthly, costing only 10 Oere (1d.). This paper, too, meets with scarcely any support within the Party. From seven clubs with a membership of about 450, during the years 1903-1906 the " Union " grew to

300-400 clubs with a membership of 14,000-15,000. At the end of 1906 the " Union " numbered 25,000 members and numerous local organizations are attached to it. The *Fram* has a circulation of 35,000-40,000 copies. The Socialist " Union " has about 10,000 members ; the *Brand* (which is much smaller than the *Fram* and its contents not so good) has a circulation of 10,000-12,000 copies.

Both Unions, in accordance with their statutes, have inscribed anti-militarist propaganda on their banners ; it is carried on especially by means of printed matter. Under the auspices of the Social-Democratic Union the " Socialdemokratiska Ungdoms förbundets Förlag " at Malmoe publishes numerous pamphlets, among others : " Ned med Vapnen " (" Down with Arms ! ") by Z. Hoeglund, and " Socialdemokrati och Anarchism " by Kate Dalstroem. According to the *Fram*, March, 1906, an onslaught was made on the military expenditure in order that the money thus wasted could be used for the benefit of " the small agricultural concerns, for educating the masses and insuring the workers " ! When the Union (between Sweden and Norway) was passing through a crisis the Social-Democratic Young People's Union (at its first Congress held at Stockholm in 1905), amongst other things discussed in an admirable manner the military question and issued the well-known appeal, " Down with Arms ! " which called upon the proletariat to refuse to do military service in the case of a war with Norway ; Comrade Z. Hoeglund had to undergo nine months' imprisonment in connection with it. The Liberal ministry, at the head of which was Staaf, the " half-Socialist "—just as in France the " Socialist " Millerand and recently the Clémenceau-Briand-Viviani ministry—at once accepted the challenge and in this way acknowledged the importance of the movement. In May, 1906, the notorious Anarchist, or muzzling, law was passed, of which we shall speak elsewhere, and it soon rained severe sentences : on 27th September, 1906, Sundstroem was condemned to one year's imprisonment (hard labour) by the municipal court at Norrkoeping for publishing a carefully-worded leaflet addressed to young men liable to military service. In addition to anti-militarist demonstrations among the soldiers this sentence gave rise—two days later—to an impressive protest demonstration held at Norrkoeping; the police resorted to force to disperse it. But this sentence produced another highly amusing effect which confirmed the truth of the proverb : " To him from whom God takes away an office, He gives back the senses." Staaf did not enjoy the glory of being a minister for long. The cold winds of the winter when he had fallen into disfavour brought him to his senses ; the fire of class justice which he, as minister, had eagerly fanned into flame, he endeavoured to extinguish as a plain citizen with buckets full of a lawyer's eloquence. In December, 1906, he undertook the defence of Comrade Sundstroem when his appeal was heard before the superior court at Joenkoeping ; he endeavoured to prove to the court that the law had not been properly interpreted. Indeed, the sentence was reduced to six months ! In the summer of 1906 followed the conviction of Comrade Olsson, who was sentenced by the municipal court at Joenkoeping to six months' imprisonment for having written an anti-militarist leaflet, " To Smaland's Young Workers." At the end of September the Young Socialist Union arranged anti-militarist demonstrations at Helsingborg and Bjuf to give a reception to the men transferred to the reserve and disbanded ; the police intervened, drawing their weapons. Many of those who had participated in the Helsingborg demonstration of 29th September were sentenced by the municipal court to thirteen months'-three years' penal servitude at the end of October. These are very promising beginnings which, however, can only influence the form and not the character and success of the anti-militarist propaganda in Sweden.

On 14th October, 1906, interesting negotiations which referred especially to the question of anti-militarism were carried on between the two Unions in regard to unity between the two organizations.

NORWAY.

Local Young Socialist organizations have existed in Norway for years, for instance at Christiania, Drammen, Larvik and Trondhjem. Since June, 1901, the " Kristiania Socialdemokratiske Ungdomslag " has published the excellent monthly, *Det Tyvende Aarhundrede*, which advocates also anti-militarism ; later it was turned into a quarterly.* A Federation of the Young Socialist organizations (" Norges Socialdemokratiske Ungdomsforbund "), with headquarters at Christiania, was founded at the congress at Drammen in June, 1903. It is believed to have a membership of about 2000, including many females. The Federation publishes a monthly called the *Jung-Socialist*, edited by Solberg ; the aim of the Federation is the furtherance of general, social and political education, and especially the struggle against militarism. Its standpoint regarding militarism is identical with that of the Social-Democratic Party. At the congress of the Federation at Whitsuntide, 1905, the motion that the anti-militarist fight *in every form* be taken up as one of its special objects was rejected.

As regards the anti-militarist agitation carried on by the Federation we should mention the pamphlet " Militarism " by Michael Puntervold, a Norwegian lieutenant ; it was disseminated widely in the garrison towns. Further, a recent occurrence should be related.

On 10th October, 1906, at Christiania, an anti-militarist meeting was called by the Social-Democratic Young People's Association. It was announced by means of leaflets distributed in all the barracks, with the heading, " Hereby the mobilization of all officers and privates is ordered." In spite of the prohibition on the part of the military authorities the meeting was well attended. Sundstroem and also Lieutenant Puntervold (who is, by the way, one of the editors of the *Socialdemokraten*) spoke at the meeting (this fact can be regarded as characteristic), though, it is true, Lieutenant

---

* The present editor is Jacob Vidnes ; it appears to be again published as a monthly ; *vide* also the following : the *Fram*, March, 1906.

Puntervold had at the time already handed in his resignation. Einar Li, another editor of the same paper, who had refused to join the army and was being persecuted in consequence under the criminal law, was also one of the speakers.

DENMARK.

In Denmark, likewise, the Young Socialist organizations are the chief supporters of anti-militarist propaganda. They sprang up to counteract the reactionary Young People's Associations, especially the Christian Young People's Associations, which had a very large membership. The first Young Socialist organization came into existence in Jutland in 1893 or 1894, but it did not become prominent until the end of the 'nineties. About the end of the century numerous Social-Democratic " Fremskridtsklebber " grew up in the smaller places in Jutland, remaining in close touch with one another.

An " Ungdomsforening " (Young People's Society) was founded at Copenhagen in 1900. In the spring of 1904 the local organizations in Copenhagen founded the " Socialistik Ungdomsfoerbund i Danmark," which publishes a monthly paper, *Ny Tid* (*New Times*). Originally the Federation was incorporated in the (Social-Democratic) Party, and was connected with the organizations of Sweden and Norway. At the time the Federation was founded it comprised nineteen local groups ; the country was divided into three propaganda districts and the Federation devoted special attention to anti-militarist propaganda. Of the appeals—which have to be printed in Sweden since no printer can be found to print them in Denmark—fifteen were confiscated one after the other, but were soon returned. As it was urged in militarist quarters that a militarist Young People's Society be founded, anti-militarist agitation on an extensive scale was begun in April, 1906. In addition to propaganda meetings 50,000 copies of the *Ny Tid* were distributed all over the country, especially among the soldiers returning after their leave of absence; of course, confiscations and arrests took place in connection therewith.

The Socialist Union gradually ran into an Anarchistic channel, and this in a more marked manner than its counterpart in Sweden. The congress of 20th-21st April, 1905, at which seven clubs with about 500 members were represented, adopted an openly antagonistic attitude towards the Social-Democratic Party, an attitude, however, which is believed not to correspond to the attitude taken up by the individual clubs, but which was the cause of a Social-Democratic Young People's club being founded at Copenhagen whose aim, in the first place, is the instruction and education of young workers, and fighting of Capitalism and Anarchism; its organization is allied to the Party. The Party Congress held at Easter, 1906, advocated the founding of similar organizations throughout the country and guaranteed them its moral and material support.

AMERICA.

There are the following facts to report concerning the *United States of America* :—

The programme of the Social-Democratic Workers' Party of North America, founded in 1874, does not include anything that refers directly to militarism; the latter had not yet made itself very conspicuous. In 1879, after the strike battle described above had been fought several workers' military societies were founded by the Socialists of Chicago and Cincinnati, under the influence of Bakunin's ideas; they were called " Educacational and Defensive Societies," but were strenuously opposed by the Party.

During the succeeding interval opinions differed greatly as to the tactics to be adopted towards the army and the militia. The Trade Unions especially made the attempt to keep aloof all members of the standing army and the militia on account of the frequent intervention of these military organizations in strikes. Others were

F

of the opinion that it was precisely by getting into closer touch with the members of the armed forces that the danger emanating from the military would be minimized.*

The Socialist Party of the United States regards both anti-militarism and anti-clericalism as problems of secondary importance to the Labour movement. It treats militarism not as an insignificant question but as a subsidiary one, and is firmly bent upon preventing the Party from becoming a mere anti-militarist organization.

Lee observes that although up to the present, *i.e.*, to the year 1905, but little Socialist propaganda work has been done among the soldiers and the militiamen, the Party has, at any rate, begun that kind of agitation.

It is significant to find in the Chicago programme of the Socialist Party of 1904 the following demand in the list of minimum demands, under paragraph 5 : " Prevention of the employment of the military against workmen on strike " ; stress is also laid upon the international solidarity of the workers.†

SPAIN.

From Spain, too, there is not much to report. Owing to the generally confused conditions in the Party want of clearness, splits, confusion and Anarchism are apparently the predominant features of the Young Socialist organizations as well as of anti-militarist agitation. There is, however, one Young Socialist organization recognized by the Social-Democratic Party, the " Federacion Nacional de Juventudes Socialistas " (National Federation of Young Socialists) with its central committee in the industrial town of Bilbao. According to the statutes printed in 1906 its aims are : Education in accordance with Socialist principles and the employment in the Party of the young people thus educated.

---

* Lee, *Vie Socialiste*, No. 18, p. 90.
† During the Dutch Anarchist Anti-Militarist Congress at Zwolle in 1904 (discussed elsewhere) a letter was received from New York, also an expression of sympathy from the National Trade Union and Labour Congress in Canada,— *Vide* the *Ontwaking*, 4th year, December, 1904.

Finland.

In the spring of 1906 a club for young workers, a branch of the Swedish Workers' Association, was founded at Helsingfors, which was immediately joined by forty members. On 10th March, 1906, the club—whose membership had, in the meantime, grown to seventy—discussed the proposal put forward by the *Fram* concerning affiliation with the Association in the kingdom of Sweden. Although the proposal was sympathetically received, for reasons of policy it was negatived for the time being. The club published a propaganda paper called the *Kamrat*. It advocated the formation of more clubs in the country and also of a union which should embrace the Finnish organizations. The first congress of the Finnish Young Socialist organizations was held at Tammerfors on 9th December, 1906 ; the affiliation of the " Union of Young Workers " of Finnish nationality to the Labour Party was resolved upon and (the resolve) " to fight against militarism in all its forms," was added to the statutes.

Russia.

Russia is a subject by itself and cannot be discussed in detail here. A few general remarks have already been made. One cannot too often point out that the position of an officer as regards the Russian revolution is quite different from that of an officer as regards the Labour movement. Thus the standpoint taken up by Plekhanov in the " Tagebuch eines Sozialdemokraten " (" Diary of a Social-Democrat), No. 7, maintaining that it is necessary to carry on an agitation amongst the officers, is in itself consistent. The anti-militarist movement in Russia is of extreme importance : it becomes one with the boundlessness of the great Revolution.

The International Anti-Militarist Organization.

Apparently the holding of an international anti-militarist congress was first suggested in 1902 by French

Anarchists with a view to establishing an international anti-militarist association. The chief motive was the desire to put upon a firm footing the maintenance of deserters abroad who crossed the frontiers in fairly large numbers in consequence of Anarchist propaganda. Most of the supporters of the idea of such a congress belonged to the " Ligue internationale pour la défense du Soldat," discussed above, which presents an unsuccessful attempt at an international anti-militarist organization on the basis of a programme too narrow in its scope. It is alleged that the idea found support in England and other countries ; a committee was formed, to all appearances under the guiding influence of Nieuwenhuis. The watchword under which the congress was called together was as " expressive " as it could possibly be : " Not a man nor a cent for militarism."

Meanwhile the agitation for the congress which was originally to be held in London in March or April, 1903, bore but little fruit, although the committee had approached even the Social-Democratic organizations (of course vainly), the Belgian " Young Guards,"* and all and sundry religious and humanitarian anti-militarists trying to induce them to attend the Congress.

After it had again become necessary to postpone indefinitely the congress which was to have been held at Amsterdam in September, 1903, a special organ, *L'Ennemi du Peuple*, was founded in Paris† for the purpose of agitating in favour of a congress. The first issue of *L'Ennemi du Peuple* appeared in August, 1903, and was edited by Janvion, the Anarchist, in a spirit of most extreme Stirnerism. At last, in June, 1904, thanks above all to the strenuous effort of Nieuwenhuis, they were able to hold the congress at Amsterdam,

---

* They were assured by Nieuwenhuis that there would be room within the League even for Social-Democratic organizations if they would not take fright at any consequences of the struggle against militarism and would recognize the above-named watchword. At the congress of the Young Guards in 1903 such participation was rejected unanimously without a discussion, because the congress did not consider this basis sufficiently firm and clear, and looked upon an international association against militarism outside the Socialist International as unnecessary and liable to cause confusion.

† " The Enemy of the People," after Ibsen's drama.

which was attended by a fairly large number of delegates. It was, to be sure, a motley company that had assembled : Anarchists of all shades from Holland, France, Belgium, Bohemia (representatives of a small group of miners), several representatives of Spanish Anarchist Trade Unions, Dutch Tolstoyans, the Evangelical pastor Schermerhorn and other varieties of religious and humanitarian anti-militarism in Holland, and, finally, several English Trade Unionists.*

It was only with difficulty that the congress was prevented from constituting itself an expressly Anarchist congress for the purpose of founding an Anarchist League. The proceedings naturally began with the expulsion of the Anarchist Individualists†, and showed that the warring elements could not be induced to take common action.

The Tolstoyans and Humanitarians were expelled, and those who remained passed several resolutions :

1. A resolution put forward by the Dutch delegates, which, whilst drawing special attention to the intervention of the military in strikes, lays down as the duty of the Trade Unions to fight militarism on principle, to establish friendly relations with the soldiers, and especially to keep in constant touch with those Trade Union members who have been called up.

2. The resolution put forward by Girault (France), which proposes that Trade Unions should found Young People's organizations for the purpose of anti-militarist propaganda work.

3. The resolution put forward by Vohryzeck (Bohemia), which recommends to the Trade Unions " of the whole world " the tactics of the French Trade Unions.‡

---

* According to the *Ontwaking*, August, 1904, p. 186, they represented 116,000 English miners of Durham and Northumberland ! The above-mentioned Spanish Trade Unionists were, according to the same source, delegated by the Spanish Trade Union Federation and represented " at least 100,000 workers " !

† Who protested against resolutions being passed in any form and naturally did not submit to the resolution of the congress to pass resolutions.

‡ This decision was to have been put into execution by the Oxford congress.

4. A Dutch resolution proclaiming the general strike as the means for opposing war.

5. Another Dutch resolution demanding anti-militarist education of the young especially by influencing the mothers.

6. Lastly, a French resolution concerning individual refusals to serve.

Thus we see there was no scarcity of resolutions. In addition a lengthy manifesto was adopted ; its blurred ideological character has been criticized by Nieuwenhuis himself with laudable severity.

All the same, the International Anti-Militarist Association was founded, and with that splendid watchword, " Not a man, nor a cent for the army." Nieuwenhuis was appointed secretary. At the same time it was decided to hold a second congress at Oxford in 1905.

The Oxford Congress was never held and just as little success attended the attempt to hold a similar congress at Geneva in June, 1906.

Amongst other things, the following items under paragraph 2 were on the agenda of the congress which was to be held at Geneva :

(*a*) What are we to do to prevent war ?

(*b*) What are we to do if a war breaks out ?

(*c*) What are anti-militarists to do if during a war the workers of a country refuse to take up arms whilst their brothers in the enemy state make an armed attack upon their country ?

(*d*) The attitude of the workers of neutral countries in the case of war.

The problem of international disarmament and of Hervéism is here presented in its practical significance with all desirable frankness.

Paragraph 3 reads as follows : anti-militarism, partial strikes and the social general strike for the establish1.ent of a communist society.

Owing to the efforts of Nieuwenhuis an anti-militarist congress was held at Zwolle in October, 1904. Nieuwenhuis made a very optimistic report on the position of the International Association and stated, among other things, that besides the *Ennemi du Peuple* a paper *L'Action Anti-Militariste* had been founded in Marseilles. The congress further resolved to found a Dutch national anti-militarist society as a branch of the International Association.

It was alleged that the Association grew very quickly in France. A national congress was held at Etienne in July, 1905, in which, according to the report of the "A.I.A.," "numerous groups took part." It was resolved to form a National Committee and to publish a national organ which, however, did not appear until 1st October, 1906, since when it has been published as a monthly in Paris under the title "*L'A.I.A.*" (the first letters of the name of the organization), as a bulletin of the Association. The congress further resolved that in case of war the reservists should strike and the soldiers refuse to obey orders and to mutiny; in the case of a general strike energetic support was to be given to the fighting Labour organizations. Desertion was not included among the acts advocated by the Association; moreover, all material responsibility in cases of desertion was repudiated, save in exceptional cases. What, above all, was of importance was the resolution, not to bind the Association to any party "doctrine," either Anarchist or Socialist, but to preserve its independent, non-party revolutionary character; insurrection was laid down as a duty in case it should be decided upon by the Association, and—taking part in elections was vetoed; the latter betrays the hoof of Anarchism. The Paris National Committee publishes in Paris, in addition to the bulletin, "Publications of the A.I.A.,"* amongst which is a pamphlet, published in 1906, concerning the aim, means and action of the A.I.A.† The

---

* Among others, the paper *La Rue* devoted to fighting Tsarism; a leaflet addressed to mothers ("A' l honneur militaire"); and the pamphlets "Lettre a un conscrit" (Letter to a Conscript), by Merle, and "La vache à lait" (The Milch Cow) letter to a Saint-Cyrien (pupil of the School for Officers at Saint Cyr) by Georges Yvetot.

† "L'A.I.A., son but, ses moyens, son action."

well-known leaflet, "Aux conscrits " (" To Conscripts " !)
on which the Paris jury wreaked its vengeance on 31st
December, 1905, was signed by the members of the
National Committee. As far as can be gathered from
the bulletins, there exists a considerable number of
local groups ("sections"); but from their financial
position one can draw the inference that their membership
is not large. The pamphlet mentioned above concerning
the aim, means and action of the Association characterizes it thus briefly : " It is a fighting organization ;
of its members it demands, in a given case, readiness for
direct, violent and rebellious action. Its only care and
the only aim of its activity is : to oppose militarism by
the will to revolt—the power that should destroy it
wherever possible." Thus it is Anarchism and insur-
rectionism after all. This is also made apparent by
the singular discussion concerning the " reproach "
levelled at the Association, that it is *an organization.**

In Switzerland, too, there exist sections of the A.I.A.

During the sitting of the International Congresses at
Paris in 1900 and at Amsterdam in 1904 respectively,
international conferences of the Young Socialists were
held. On each occasion they asked the national council
of the Belgian Young Guards to establish an international connection, but it was never carried out.

An international connection between the Young
Socialist organizations has thus so far been attempted
in vain. It is, however, in all probability, not far off.

---

* " L'A.I.A.," pp. 15-16.

DANGERS BESETTING ANTI-MILITARISM.

REACTION and capitalism are especially sensitive as regards militarism. They have fully recognized that when they defend militarism they defend their chief position of power *versus* democracy and the working class : they stand opposed to anti-militarism of both kinds as a solid phalanx, that is to say, in so far as anti-militarism is directed against the militarism against the enemy abroad and the enemy at home. The golden days when a wavering treatment, often harmless and merciful, was meted out to anti-militarists by justice temporarily put under the ban with the assistance of traditional revolutionary phraseology, may come to an end as regards Belgium and even France since anti-militarism has become a serious menace to the anti-proletarian powers. As regards Germany, let us recall the muzzling and stupefying decree of January, 1894, issued by von Gossler, minister of war (published in the *Reichsanzeiger*, 6th August, 1897). The non-commissioned officers and privates (not the officers whose way of thinking, thanks to their birth and social standing, can be relied upon in any case) are officially forbidden by the decree not only to engage in any recognizable activity of a revolutionary or Social-Democratic character, as well as in harbouring and spreading revolutionary and Social-Democratic writings, but also to participate in any gatherings, meetings, festivities, collections of money whatsoever without previous official sanction in order to preclude all evasion and involuntary temptation. And what is especially characteristic of the ruthlessness with which militarism pursues its ends and of the disregard it shows for the " fellow's " sense of honour and decency is the official

137

command to those in the active army to report at once
officially if it comes to their notice that revolutionary
or Social-Democratic writings are in the barracks or on
other premises used by the military. Thus German
militarism has created for itself a protection of an
especially criminal kind against the penetration of the
Social-Democratic or any anti-militarist poison in
general into the active army, even though an act *per se*
be ever so lawful and ever so far removed from incitement
to disobedience, etc. This protection surpasses even
the notorious Swedish muzzling law. Secret denuncia-
tion which is everywhere looked upon as a most dastardly
thing here becomes an official command ; he who does
not denounce is imprisoned for disobeying official
orders ! What fills the cup to overflowing is that it is
implicitly laid down in the above-mentioned decree that
these prohibitions and commands apply also to the
persons called up for training or for inspection. It is
simply impossible to control and to enforce that the men
called up for training or for inspection should, for
instance, sever their connection with the Trade Unions
and other so-called revolutionary organizations for the
duration of the training or even for the duration of the
day on which the inspection takes place, or that they
discontinue their subscriptions to the Labour papers
for this interval (a thing technically impossible), or even
that they, during this interval, refrain from reading the
forbidden revolutionary literature and banish it from
their dwellings. Nevertheless a case relating to 1905 is
known to the author in which the court martial of
Potsdam sentenced a workman to a long term of imprisonment because, in the evening of the day when the
inspection had taken place, he had also taken part in a
Trade Union meeting. On the other hand, an action
started against a workman in 1904 by the criminal court
of Potsdam failed ; the workman had sent a Social-
Democratic paper to a non-commissioned officer he knew
which dealt with the bad material conditions of the
non-commissioned officers ; but in this case he was
acquitted.

How rigorously Gossler's decree is being applied to the men on active service is proved, among other things, by the cases reported of soldiers who, in answer to an official inquiry or even as witnesses giving evidence under oath, had stated that they held Social-Democratic opinions with the cautious reservation, " in civil life," have been condemned by court martial ; this is obviously a gross illegality and an immoral thing.

Let us also recall the case of Colonel Gaedke, which is important in many respects. As an officer in the reserve he was deprived of the right of wearing his uniform because he had made the general remark when discussing the murder of the Serbian royal couple that, " Under certain conditions an officer's duty to his country should come before his duty to the monarch." The criminal prosecution by the police of the Koenigsberg Society of Apprentices and Young Workers took place in the summer of 1906. And, last but not least, there is the secret decree of the Prussian war minister published in the press at the beginning of October, 1906, which relates to ascertaining the method as well as the extent of the Social-Democratic anti-militarist propaganda ; this decree at the same time reflects the fear and bad conscience of our ruling classes. The anti-Social-Democratic instructions of General von Eichhorn also belong to this category.

This sensitiveness in regard to anti-militarism is just as international as capitalism and militarism ; and the reaction against anti-militarist activity is everywhere violent and brutal, as has been shown in another connection.

The Swedish muzzling law against anti-militarist agitation, which was carried into effect by Staaf, the " half-Socialist," in May, 1906, deserves to be more fully described. This law was passed by the first Chamber without a debate and by the second Chamber after a lively debate, but by an overwhelming majority ; we must look upon this law as being the principle in accordance with which the anti-militarists will be " legally " fought in the future. This law stiffened

considerably the normal penalties for several infringe-
ments of public order, such as the incitement to punishable actions by word of mouth or by means of the
printed word : it raised the maximum penalty from
two years' imprisonment to four years' penal servitude !
Further, it makes punishable the " laudation " of
illegal actions and incitement to disobey the law, in so far
as it is done through the medium of the press, and
makes it the duty of the military authorities to con-
fiscate writings which pursue the obvious end of undermining the sense of duty and obedience of the soldiers,
and to transmit them to a specially appointed authority.
Finally, it empowers the commanders of troops to forbid
the soldiers to attend gatherings in case it can be taken
for granted that statements would be made thereat
which might imperil discipline. The effects of this law
have already been portrayed.

Meslier* is in the right : reaction declares everywhere
that the barracks are sacrosanct and inviolable, and
treats anti-militarism everywhere as treason. But when
he says of France : " The most vehement denunciations
of anti-militarism come from the temple of the golden
calf, the Stock Exchange, from the ranks of international
capital which hypocritically raises its voice in the
interests of the fatherland," it applies to Germany up
to the present time, only with the reservation which
results from the peculiar kind of our monarchic-bureau-
cratic-agrarian capitalism.

A highly interesting proof of this sensitiveness in
regard to anti-militarism and, at the same time, of the
large extent to which the function of militarism against
the enemy abroad has taken the second place in comparison with militarism against the enemy at home, is
furnished by the utterances of the German Emperor
whose speeches made on 26th January, 1895, and on

---

* *Vide* " Un côté de la question sociale " (One Aspect of the Social Question).
Moltke said in the Reichstag on 19th March, 1869 : " Let us rejoice that we, in
Germany, have an army which only *obeys*. What we see when we look at other
countries is that the army brings on the revolution instead of the army being a
means of defence against revolution. I advise you most emphatically never to
lend a hand to the army becoming something different from what it now is in
Germany."

22nd March, 1901, contained an appeal to the effect
that the fight against the Socialist aspirations of educating the young people be taken up ; such proof is also
furnished by his utterances to the French journalist,
Gaston Menier, in 1906. The Emperor in this case
characterized anti-militarism as an "international
scourge," especially French anti-militarism, that is to
say, the anti-militarism which is alleged to be on the
point of weakening the capacity for action and the
readiness to strike of the French army, the army of our
"hereditary foe"! Another step in this direction,
and an international anti-anti-militarist league would
be founded !

CHAPTER IV

ANTI-MILITARIST TACTICS.

ANTI-MILITARISM *per se* is nothing specifically proletarian or revolutionary, just as little as militarism is anything specifically bourgeois or capitalist. We need only recall the past, for instance the Russian Decembrists and the bourgeois-nationalist " Catechism for Soldiers " by Ernst Moritz Arndt (written) in September, 1812, who called upon the soldiers openly to rebel against the traitorous princes. Decisive proof of this is furnished by the Russian revolution in more recent times. We have, however, to confine ourselves to anti-militarism in the capitalist states.

1. TACTICS AGAINST MILITARISM ABROAD.*

The final aim of anti-militarism is the abolition of militarism, that is to say, the abolition of the army in every form. Together with the army needs must fall all the other manifestations of militarism which have been described and which in reality are only the accessory effects of the existence of the army. When the house falls the roof goes with it.

This object could be achieved forthwith by the proletariat only if we presuppose such an international situation as excludes the necessity for employing the army *in the interest of the proletariat,* in which case the interests of the proletariat need in no way oppose the national interests.

The necessity for a military organization for capitalism could also be done away with, looking at it from a

---

* *Vide* the inquiry in the *Vie Socialiste,* I., Nos. 15-18 ; the *Mouvement Socialiste,* 1905 ; and *Vorwaerts,* 17th September, 1905 ; also the protocols of the international congresses.

logical point of view, by getting rid of possibilities of conflict or by international disarmament on a uniform scale.

To do away with the possibilities of conflict would, in the first place, mean renouncing the policy of expansion which, as has been shown elsewhere, may possibly come to pass in the future by the Globe becoming trustified by the Great Powers ; it would mean what, in the end, would amount to the same thing : the creation of a federal world state.

But this, for the time being, is a romantic dream concerning the future ; all probabilities point in the direction that the world policy will not attain this " state of permanency " until the proletariat attains its final aim and replaces the capitalist world policy by its own.

And matters are still worse as regards international disarmament. It not only signifies that militarist rivalry has to be abandoned by the military states, but also that the chances of gain of the most powerful states would have to be surrendered. (From this arises the proposal for arbitration in regard to establishing contingents in proportion to the individual armies.) Disarmament means neither less nor more than the surrender of the international interests which might induce the ruling classes, capitalism, to appeal to the *ultima ratio regum*, that is to say, exactly such interests as are regarded by capitalism as highly important, in fact its very life interests, especially the policy of expansion. The belief that all this can be carried out under the domination of capitalism before that natural political state of permanency throughout the world has been attained, is mere superstition. Of course the influence which runs counter to the world policy and favours a world federation, the influence which is exerted by the proletariat upon foreign policy, is becoming ever stronger, even in backward countries, and may conduce to lessening the dangers of war and rendering the world policy a peaceful policy ; but the greater the influence exerted by the proletariat, the

greater becomes the danger of Bonapartist tricks, so
that it is doubtful whether the sum total of the possibilities of war may be reduced ; there can be no question
of eliminating them.

Anti-militarism, too, can be the means of bringing
about international disarmament on a uniform scale if
it succeeds in rendering the existing armies incapable
of action or, at least, in crippling their activity. Hervé
demands—and this is the essence of his ideas—that we
should work in the direction of this crippling at any
price. Many more or less weighty objections have been
raised against the feasibility of this plan. The following
is the weightiest of these objections, though it does not
apply to the proposal which involves a combination of
disarmament and of *revolution :* It is *impossible* to bring
about *complete* universal disarmament, on an international scale, for even in the most progressive countries
plenty of strike-breakers are nearly always to be found
during strikes ; precisely the civilized powers would
relatively be most weakened and thus become a ready
prey to the lower types of culture.

But Hervé's idea can be adopted even in principle
only in case the proletariat under no circumstances and
in no case has any interest in the nation being able to
defend itself. And the main dispute quite consistently
revolves around this point. In this dispute Kautsky's
standpoint of " realpolitik," which rightly is not satisfied
with a superficial and misleading differentiation between
an offensive and a defensive war, certainly deserves
preference to the overdrawn anti-patriotism of the
Yonne Federation which fails to recognize the practical
position : Until the economic and social state of permanency striven after by Social-Democracy and the
abolition of the class character of society have been
realized internationally there exist possibilities of war
from which even Social-Democracy cannot shut itself
out. It goes without saying, as has been mentioned
elsewhere, that the regular causes of war under capitalism
are so constituted that the proletariat has nothing to do
with them, moreover must oppose them with all its

might. For all that, it is incorrect to think that all wars are acts directed against the proletariat. In a Bonapartist sense this is certainly possible ; and there may certainly be a bit of Bonapartism " present all the time." But what, as a rule, is essential about the causes of war connected with the world policy is the fight for spoils, for profit between the capitalist classes of the world powers. Of course, insurrections and revolutions may break out in consequence of and in the course of such wars, and the necessity may be forced upon every one of the belligerent powers to turn the weapons against their own proletariat ; thus the solidarity of the ruling classes of the belligerent powers as opposed to the proletariat is brought about : but this in most cases would tend to lead to a termination of the war. And it is just as natural that every lucky war due to capitalist motives, whether pre-conceived or not, produces Bonapartist effects ; whereas, if the war takes an unfavourable course the certain damage done to culture is, at any rate, balanced by the possibility that the capitalist reaction may be overthrown. Thus the proletariat has a powerful incentive to work against war, and it becomes a thing easy to conceive and almost to be commended, that here and there the mark is overshot in the fight against war. Hervéism as an awakener and inciter of thought has a valuable mission to fulfil and fulfils it.

We must first make a distinction according to the kind of war. . . . This will show in what cases disarmament is to be striven after on principle.

Of course, the question of the attitude to be taken towards war on principle is of the greatest practical importance and is no mere theoretical speculation. Nor does it present its own solution when we have a concrete case before us ; on the contrary, it is precisely such a concrete case which, owing to the excitement of the situation, easily brings with it the tendency to blur one's clear insight. The events in Germany which took place within the Party when the Franco-German war and the Herero rebellion broke out warn us to be on our guard and to clear up the question of principle betimes. Further, it is necessary to examine in each case, apart from the question of what is desirable on principle, what can be achieved in practice. And in this respect, too, Hervé cherishes dangerous illusions. The time is not yet ripe for a general strike and for a military strike against *every* war injurious to the working class. Hervé exclaims : " Energetic anti-militarist and anti-patriotic agitation, and the mountain will come to Mahomed ! " Here Hervé shows his Anarchist colours. We contend that the overwhelming mass of the proletariat is not yet class-conscious and not yet enlightened in the Social-Democratic sense ; how then can the proletariat be expected to resort to anti-patriotic action in a case which not only requires readiness for sacrifice and sang-froid, but also presence of mind in the whirl of a furious Chauvinist surge. Complete success cannot be attained ; the measure of success, of disarmament, will be in direct proportion to the measure of education and training which fall to the share of the working class in every country : the most backward nation will be the best able to defend itself. An action of this kind would be a premium upon cultural backwardness so long as the training of the broad mass of the proletariat and its readiness for the struggle in the countries drawn into war is not almost uniformly raised to the highest possible point. Organization and universal revolutionary enlightenment of Labour are the preliminary conditions for a successful general and military strike in case of war. It would be fantastic to employ merely anti-militarist propaganda to this end.

In a normal case things stand thus : When the proletariat has got as far as being able to carry out such acts it has progressed far enough to capture political power. There are no more unfavourable conditions for displaying proletarian power than those which obtain normally when war breaks out.

And as regards Hervé's plan of combining the military strike with insurrection, that is, the attempt to capture political power and to render the revolution capable of

defending itself, from the purely logical point of view
it would not be a premium upon cultural backwardness. It would only be necessary to ask whether such a
plan (to the extent that such a thing is at all possible
in a social revolution) can be realized on a *national*
scale, quite apart of the question of doing it on an
international scale as proposed by those who advocate
the mere military strike or general strike. The possibility of realizing it on a national scale stands, first of
all, in direct proportion to the development of the proletariat and the degree of the political, social and
economic pressure under which it lives. And this
pressure will either act as a brake or will accelerate
things in accordance with its intensity and the manner
in which it affects the economic, political, and intellectual development of the proletariat. So that in
countries with a moderate pressure, in spite of a
high proletarian development — as, for instance, in
England—not more would be attained than in territories with a high pressure and a low proletarian
development—as, for instance, in the agricultural and
in the overwhelmingly Catholic industrial districts of
Germany. What may be practicable for France,
Belgium and Switzerland, is not practicable for Germany
by a long way. And mere anti-militarist propaganda
certainly cannot supply that which is lacking, even if
such propaganda is excellently suited to awaken class-
consciousness. There is the further objection : Even
insurrections *cannot be made*. If we reason intelligently
and calmly we cannot assume that *every* war (or even a
war which is condemned by the proletariat and which
is injurious to it), even if agitation were carried on in
the most energetic manner, would straightway raise the
mass of the people—even of the nation in the best
position, let alone all the nations exploited by capitalism
—to revolutionary fever heat which would be the proviso
for a successful revolt.

War is a thing which nowhere takes place so regularly
as does the conflict with political militarism at home ;
it generally presents itself to the consciousness of the

masses as a future danger of rather a theoretical kind. War is no pure manifestation of the class-struggle, self-evident to the masses, and its dependence upon the actions of foreign states renders it more difficult to take stock of it, as well as of the undertakings directed against it.

In this case, too, Hervé underrates the important driving forces which would have to be employed by such anti-war action if it should not collapse in a ridiculous and at the same time dangerous way, like a bomb bursting in the pocket of him who was about to throw it.

Again the question is: *Distinguo !* Don't measure everything with the same yard measure !

Of course there are wars which let loose the revolutionary forces which create a powerful social and political tension within individual states and bring it to a snapping point. To this category belongs the case of an intervention in Russia,* whose feasibility, it is true, is rather remote. The outbreak of such a war would be the signal for the peoples of Western Europe to commence the most ruthless class war ; it would be a pressure, the blow of a whip that would cause an uprising against reaction at home, against the worshippers of the knout, against the foul executioners of an unhappy people thirsting for freedom. Indeed, Vaillant's war-cry : " *Plutôt l'insurrection que la guerre,*" would find an enthusiastic echo among the proletariat of all civilized countries.

One can already to-day perceive other cases in which such a solidarity ready for sacrifice would spring up spontaneously ; for instance, in a war between Sweden and Norway. But this is not a normal development on which we have to base the principles of our tactics. It is possible that within measureable time such a situation may be created by a war between France and Germany. It is up to Social-Democracy of both countries to hasten on the coming of this period of solidarity by doing revolutionary work of enlightenment. Of course

---

* Germany's intervention in Russia to assist the Tsar in crushing the Revolution.—*Trans.*

much depends upon the cause of a war ; it cannot be denied, for instance, that in spite of all efforts to create an atmosphere in favour of the world policy, the colonial causes of war which are particularly real to-day bring but little grist to the mill of those interested in war.

If, for the time being, we can set complete dis-armament as our object only in exceptional cases, there are no practical reasons, or reasons of principle, against relative disarmament which merely reduces the readiness of an army for *attack*. The abolition of the standing army and the substitution of a citizen army, of a militia, and the corresponding reduction of the army expenditure (which goes hand in hand with it and which has been demonstrated by Gaston Moch in an expert manner) and the weakening of all the other baneful militarist influences*—these are the demands which the class-conscious proletariat has quite con-sistently inscribed everywhere upon its banner.

Accordingly, there are good reasons why the decisions of the international congresses (which contain the minimum anti-militarist programme of the majority of the organizations which endorse the principles of the modern Labour movement) contain only generalities in regard to " militarism against the enemy abroad." Accordingly, in no less degree is the fact justified that the tactical programmes of the individual national parties fail, almost everywhere, to specify their action in regard to this aspect of militarism, and that the struggle against militarism, as a rule, takes place in the arena of general politics ; the struggle is carried on by the national parties in such a way that they attempt to get nearer their object by exerting an influence on the whole social order without striving overmuch after specializing their propaganda. The resolution moved by Vaillant at the French party conference at Limoges, which is to be submitted to the

---

* *Vide* Moch's " The Army of Democracy " ; *vide* also Bebel's " Not a Stand-ing Army but a Citizen Army," p. 44 and following, and Berner's " Man-Killing Militarism," p. 52 and following, quoted by Bebel ; " Handbook for Social-Democratic Electors," 1903, p. 20 and following.

Stuttgart congress in 1907, is, in its main features, good
and serviceable.
The attacks by the Anarchists, especially by Nieuwenhuis, upon this attitude of Social-Democracy are bound
to fail. Though the resolution may betray a certain
helplessness it is not bombastic ; moreover, the attitude
of those is bombastic and fantastic who by advertising
unrealizable schemes attempt to solve the tactical
problem which to-day cannot be solved in its entirety.

2. Tactics Against Militarism at Home.

The question concerning the struggle against
" militarism at home " is much simpler. The struggle
is far more promising of success and its self-evident aim
is disarmament, the unconditional and effective disarmament of the state power. The method of the struggle
which most readily adjusts itself to the political conditions in individual countries lies between the slow,
calm and thorough work of enlightenment and that of
the French, whose war-cry is : " *Soldats, vous ne tirerez
pas!* " (" Soldiers, don't shoot ! ").
This struggle and the necessity for specializing it is
being forced upon the proletariat the whole time,
especially in those countries where the employment of
the military against workers on strike or against workers
who hold political demonstrations is the order of the
day. In France and Belgium, Italy, Switzerland,
Austria and everywhere one can trace plainly how the
specialized anti-militarist propaganda receives its special
form and becomes an actuality under the pressure of
military intervention in the class struggle. And this
applies to France in spite of Hervéism, whose large
number of adherents in the Syndicalist movement can
be put down to its anti-patriotic tendency only in a very
small degree. It applies also to America as has been
testified by Lee.* And if in Germany just this particular
kind of anti-militarist propaganda encounters widespread

---

* *Vie Socialiste*, No. 18, p. 80.

apathy, this is in no small degree due to the fact that in this country the intervention of the armed military forces in strikes, accompanied by bloodshed, has been practically avoided. Is it also going to be the inevitable fate of progressive popular movements to cover up the well after the child has fallen in? Is even Social-Democracy going to remain deaf to all the Cassandra calls, though it has a programme which looks joyfully and clearly far into the future?

3. ANARCHIST AND SOCIAL-DEMOCRATIC ANTI-MILITARISM.

The Social-Democratic aim is deduced from an economico-historical conception ; *only therein* does it find its justification and it is, therefore, far removed from all Utopianism. The aim of Anarchism is ideologically construed without a historical basis : this indicates the relation and the contrast between the two movements.

The Social-Democratic conception is historically organic ; the Anarchist conception is arbitrarily mechanical. Anarchism, it is true, regards men as the bearers of evolution as understood by it, and their will as the agent, and accordingly it sets itself the task of influencing this will. Social-Democracy, too, regards influencing the will of the workers as its task.

But for all that, there exist differences of the most fundamental character.

For Anarchism, influencing the will is the only essential preliminary condition of success ; for Social-Democracy it is only of secondary importance by the side of the objective economic stages of development, none of which can be skipped over, even with the best will of the masses and of a class.

The Anarchists consider it always possible to exert such an influence if enough energy be expended. Social-Democracy considers it possible as a mass and class manifestation only in so far as a certain predisposition exists which has been created by the economic situation. Both conceptions wage their dispute around the necessity

for this predisposition, while the differences within
Social-Democracy spring chiefly from the doubt as to
whether this predisposition is existent in a given case.
Naturally it is difficult to decide the question whether
the economic conditions are ripe for action, and it is
difficult to establish the measure in which the will
should be influenced, especially the measure of predisposition which is indispensable in an individual case ;
personal optimism or pessimism and temperament here
play an important *rôle*. From this arise the differences
within Social-Democracy : those who assume that this
influence can be exerted in a greater degree and demand
only a small degree of predisposition approach Anarchism : these are the Anarchist-Socialists. In spite of
the contrast—which is not contradictory—between
Anarchism and Socialism we, therefore, find all possible
gradations, like the colours in the spectrum, between
these two tendencies.

The degree to which the will can be influenced depends
upon the degree of predisposition and upon the unstability of the mental equilibrium of the people or the
class to be influenced. This unstability in times of
excitement is immeasurably greater than in times of
quiet : hence there is a potentiality which acts like a
will-o'-the-wisp at times in a confusing way ; it is
sometimes downright dangerous, but in most cases it
is a highly valuable potentiality, that is to say, more
can be achieved in times of excitement than in times of
quiet ; but it is a surplus which, as soon as quiet is
restored, nearly always is lost again, at least, to a certain
extent, together with the surplus of energy which it
helped to generate : the history of revolutions is the
only continuous confirmation of this fact.

The fundamental difference between the two basic
conceptions manifests itself also therein that Anarchism
regards it as possible for a mere handful of resolute
men to accomplish everything—of course, by making
use of the will of the masses which remain either active
or passive. Of course, Socialism also holds the view
that a resolute and capable minority with a clear aim

in view can carry the masses with it in decisive moments
and exert a great influence. But this is the difference :
while Socialism strives after exerting such influence and
looks upon it as feasible only in the sense that this
minority awakens and carries out the will of the masses,
that will which, owing to a particular situation, the
masses are ready and capable of displaying as their
social will, Anarchism does it after the fashion of a true,
enlightened despotism, in the sense that a resolute
handful of usurpers only carry out their own will and
make use of the masses as a tool towards this end.

Anarchism tries to spring, on an untamed horse, over
the difficulties which have their root in the economic
and social conditions or, according to circumstances, to
bridle the horse upside down. Its underlying idea is :
In the beginning was the deed. Of course a period may
come in the development of the class struggle when the
action proposed by Anarchism will be feasible and
correct. But the fault of Anarchism lies not in the
absolute impracticability of its methods, but in their
relative impracticability which arises from the fact that
Anarchism fails to see the social correlation of power
at a given time ; this in its turn is due to a lack of
historical and social insight. And if the proposals of
Anarchism can be realized in the *later* stages of development and approved of, this is no justification, but on
the contrary, a condemnation of Anarchist tactics ;
to do the tactics justice one must say, however,
that their merit lies in the fact that they often stimulate
thought.

Anarchist and Anarchistic anti-militarism is related
to the Anarchist and Anarchistic general strike, it is a
twin-brotherhood outwardly recognizable by the fact
that for this kind of anti-militarism the military strike
is invariably the culminating point. To grasp the
essence of this kind of anti-militarism and to recognize
the difference between it and Social-Democratic anti-
militarism the following things must be kept apart :
the cause of anti-militarism, the method of propagating
anti-militarism, the final aim and object which are to be

attained by anti-militarism, and the method by which anti-militarism seeks to attain this object.

The cause of the anti-militarist movement is the same both from the point of view of Anarchism and of Social-Democracy in so far as both regard militarism as a special obstacle of a mechanical and violent character to the realization of their social plans. But otherwise the cause is as different to one and the other as are the Anarchist and the Social-Democratic conceptions of the world. We cannot describe here more fully how little consistency there is in the Anarchist conception of the organically capitalist character of militarism and, therefore, of the laws of the economic and social development to be applied to it. Here lies the root of all the other essential differences between the Socialist and Anarchist anti-militarism, which can be briefly stated as follows : the Social-Democratic anti-militarism wages the fight against militarism as a function of capitalism while recognizing the laws of the social and economic development and applying them to it. Anarchism looks upon militarism as a thing by itself, brought about in an arbitrary and accidental way by the ruling classes. Anarchism wages the fight against it, just like the fight against capitalism in general, from a fantastic ideological point of view which ignores the laws of social and economic development. In merely touching the surface Anarchism attempts to knock militarism out of the saddle by appealing to the resolution of the individual, which is not rooted in the social and economic development ; in short, it does it in an individualist manner. Anarchism is not only individualistic in its social aim— in a varying degree—but even in its historical, social and political conception and in its methods.

The final aim both of Anarchist and Social-Democratic anti-militarism if we are satisfied with a mere war-cry is the same : complete abolition of militarism. Social-Democracy, however, in accordance with its conception of the essence of militarism regards the complete abolition of militarism alone as impossible : militarism can only fall together with capitalism—the last system of class society. Capitalism, of course, is not something constant, but a thing which continually undergoes change, which can be changed and weakened considerably by numerous counter-tendencies inherent in it, above all, proletarian tendencies. So also the life manifestation of capitalism *per se* which we call militarism in different countries, as is shown by its different forms, is not incapable of being weakened ; also its connection with capitalism can be loosened.* But this also applies, now in a greater, now in a smaller degree to the other life manifestations of capitalism and alters nothing in the organically capitalist† character of militarism, and nothing in the fact that the object of Social-Democratic anti-militarist propaganda is not fighting it as an isolated thing, and in that its final aim is not the isolated abolition of militarism ; Anarchist anti-militarist propaganda, on the contrary, regards the isolated abolition of militarism as its final aim in the plainest possible way. Of course, we cannot dispute the fact that the Anarchists, too, for the most part, wage the struggle (this, too, understood in the non-organic capitalist sense) against capitalism— but they do it on lines which run parallel (to the other propaganda)—and that even Anarchists in pursuing their theoretical course which is truly of a zigzag character infrequently show glimpses of more profound social insight.

The fundamentally different historical methods of interpretation are most apparent in the methods of the struggle. Here we must distinguish between the method of promoting an anti-militarist movement and the method of employing such a movement in opposition to militarism. As regards the first method, Anarchism works here, first of all, with ethical enthusiasm, with the stimuli of morality, with arguments of humanity, of justice ; in short, with all sorts of impulses on the will which ignore the class war character of anti-militarism, an attempt to stamp it as an abstract efflux of a cate-

---

* *Vide* in this connection p. 161 and p. 167.
† Better said : " Arising organically from the character of the systems of class society."

gorical imperative of universal application. Quite
consistently therewith it often turns its attention not
only to the men, but also to the officers.* Thus the
propaganda of Anarchist anti-militarism resembles, in a
way that brings much discredit upon it, the pathetic
declamations of Tolstoyans and the impotent incanta-
tions against war of the friends of a world peace of the
type of Bertha von Suttner.

Social-Democratic anti-militarist propaganda, on the
contrary, propagates the class-struggle and therefore it
appeals on principle exclusively to those classes which,
necessarily, are the foes of militarism in the class struggle,
though, of course, it is pleased to see the bourgeois
chips which fall to its lot in the process of disintegration.
It enlightens people to win them over, but it enlightens
them not concerning categorical imperatives, humanitarian points of view, ethical postulates of freedom and
justice, but concerning the class struggle, the interests
of the proletariat therein, the *rôle* of militarism and the
rôle which the proletariat plays, and has to play, in the
class struggle. It deduces the tasks of the proletariat
in regard to militarism from the interests of the proletariat in the class struggle. Of course, Social-Democratic
anti-militarist propaganda also applies to one's heart's
desire ethical arguments, the whole pathos of the
categorical imperative, of the elementary rights of man
and the beautiful but never practised moral principles
of the bourgeoisie from the time of its dawn, even
religious, especially Christian ideas and conceptions.
But all these play only a secondary *rôle*. They serve
the more easily to open the closed eyes of the unenlightened proletarians so that the daylight of class-
consciousness can reach their brain ; they further serve
the purpose of rousing their enthusiasm for action.

The method of applying anti-militarism, of giving
effect to anti-militarist sentiments in the case of Anarchism is again more of an individualistic and fantastic
character. It lays great stress upon individual refusal

---

* It has already been shown that in Russia the officers, too, can be reached
by anti-militarism from the standpoint of the class-war.

to do military service, individual refusal to resort to arms and upon individual protests. Anarchist literature exultingly registers all such cases with great care and exactitude. Of course, it has two objects in view: taking the action of the kind just mentioned against militarism and doing a kind of propaganda by deed on behalf of the anti-militarist movement. It starts from the premises that such heroic examples call forth imitation and awaken sympathy and enthusiasm for the principles which these " heroes " endorse.

It is different with Social-Democratic anti-militarism. Certainly it knows well that such individual acts can be, and will be, signals for and symptoms of mass movements; but they are merely signals and symptoms ; and they are signals, of course, only when tension is at its highest and most critical point, when all that needs doing is to light the fuse which connects with the gunpowder barrel. To effect a gradual organic disintegration and demoralization of the militarist spirit—this is Social-Democracy's method of fighting militarism. Everything else serves this end or plays a part only in a secondary degree. As for the rest, even in Anarchism a current which looks critically upon individual action acquires a growing and determining influence, as is shown by the International Anti-militarist Association.

The tactics of Anarchist anti-militarists are fantastic as regards the military strike which, to a certain extent, given good will and great energy they expect to conjure out of the clouds, whereas Social-Democracy regards the military strike, as any eventual incitement of the troops to take part in the revolution, merely as a logically and psychologically necessary consequence of the disintegration of the militarist spirit, which disintegration again can come about only parallel to and in consequence of the class division and of enlightenment.

The small pamphlet, " Le Militarisme,"* by Domela Nieuwenhuis, is very characteristic of Anarchist anti-militarism. For him it is not the crowned kings who

---

* *Publications des Temps Nouveaux*, No. **17**, Paris, 1901.

are the lords of the world, but the bankers, financiers and capitalists (in no way capitalism as an organically necessary social system) ; for him wars depend on the voluntary decision of the bankers ; for him reaction is the party in authority which extends " from the Pope to Karl Marx." Without examining the class position of the soldiers, he accepts in quite a general way the words of Frederic, prompted by a bad conscience : " When my soldiers have begun to think, not one of them will remain in the army." He borrows methods of anti-militarist propaganda as proposed by Laveleye in his book, " Des causes actuelles de guerre en Europe et de l'arbitrage " (" On the Actual Causes of War in Europe and on Arbitration ") :

1. Removing all restrictions on international traffic ;

2. Rendering cheaper the freight, postal and telegraph tariffs ;

3. Introduction of a uniform international system of coinage, weights and measures, and of uniform international trade legislation ;

4. Putting foreigners on a footing of equality with the native inhabitants ;

5. Promotion of the knowledge of foreign languages and of foreign cultures in general ;

6. Creation of an extensive literature embracing writings and works of art which cultivate the love of peace and hatred of war and gain adherents to the cause ;

7. Promotion of everything that gives strength and effectiveness to the representative system and can help to bring it about that the executive authority be deprived of the right to decide on war and peace ;

8. Favouring all those industrial undertakings which apply the surplus wealth of a country to increasing the natural wealth of other countries, and in such a way as to render capital cosmopolitan and thus establish a solidarity as regards the interests of international capitalists ;

9. (Nieuwenhuis raises objection only to the following point):—The clergy ought to fill the minds with a horror of war, after the fashion of the Quakers.

To these anti-militarist methods Nieuwenhuis adds others which he considers still more effective, namely :

10. Promotion of the international interests of the workers ;

11. Doing away with kings, presidents, Upper Houses, parliaments as social institutions which are inimical to peace ;

12. Abolition of ambassadorships ;

13. Reforming the teaching of history by turning it into a teaching of the history of culture ;

14. Abolition of standing armies ;

15. Settling international disputes by arbitration ;

16. The various European states to form the Federated United States of Europe after the fashion of the United States of America ;

17. A military strike and a general strike in case of war ;

18. Passive resistance and individual refusals to serve ;

19. Promotion of the general evolution and of the conditions which make for the welfare of the whole of mankind.

Here Nieuwenhuis makes the following characteristic remark : " If men have anything to lose through war it is in their interest to preserve peace," as if the proletariat were the disturber of the peace at the present time !

The careful critic will see here* nought else but confusion ; confusion in the fundamental social and historical conception, confusion in the arrangement of the subject, confusion in the conception of detail. The main point has not been mentioned at all. The most

---

* What Nieuwenhuis states in the *Ontwaking*, p. 196 and following, in criticising the manifesto of the A.I.A. congress is much clearer and has more depth.

important dealt with, namely, that which relates to
certain economic foundations of militarism, is mentioned
as a side-issue and as if by accident.   Second-rate and
third-rate points which are of quite a subsidiary character
appear in the foreground, and side by side with them
are placed quite fantastic Utopian methods.   The
means of propagating anti-militarism are lumped
together with anti-militarist action itself.   The super-
ficiality of the fundamental conception and the inclination to leave everything to personal initiative and
goodwill make themselves evident.   The last sentence
in Nieuwenhuis' booklet is a revelation of the Anarchist
conception whose very foundations are wanting in
clearness ;   it reads as follows ;   "Audacity, more
audacity, always audacity ;   this is what is necessary
that we may triumph."

CHAPTER V.

THE NEED FOR SPECIAL ANTI-MILITARIST PROPAGANDA.

CERTAINLY militarism bears in its womb many germs of self-destruction and disintegration; certainly the whole capitalist culture contains many contradictory elements which mutually tear one another to pieces, not the least of which are tendencies of a scientific, artistic and ethical formation, which make an onslaught on militarism. The undermining activity of the *Simplicissimus* literature, for instance, must in no wise be underrated.* The history of Cromwell, the history of the year 1790 in France and of the year 1806 in Germany teach us how a militarist system can become so foul and rotten that it falls to pieces of itself. Of course, in all bloody conflicts between the people and the state power, a peculiar psychology of blood becomes active and powerful, a kind of suggestion, a hypnotism of blood or even, to speak with Andreyev, a logic of blood—which may, in a moment, reverse the correlation of forces in a decisive manner. All this has no bearing upon the question of the necessity of propaganda which itself is a part of the organic process of disintegration, and the same can be said of all the other life manifestations of capitalism; all this has to be considered only in regard to the chances of a successful agitation.

The special dangerousness of militarism has been shown. The proletariat is faced by a robber armed to the teeth whose ultimatum is not, " *la bourse ou la vie* " (" Your money *or* your life "), but " *la bourse et la vie* " (" Your money *and* your life " !), which surpasses even

* Major-General von Zepelin writes in detail about this danger in the *Kreuz-zeitung*, 23rd December, 1906.

robber morality. Apart from constituting a great future
danger, militarism is a danger ever present, ever real,
even when it does not actually strike out. Militarism
is not only the Moloch of the economic life, the vampire
of the progress of culture and the chief falsifier of the
grouping into classes ; it is also the final secret or open
regulator of the form of the political and economic
movement of the proletariat, of the tactics of the class
struggle, which in all important questions is determined
by militarism as the chief pillar of the brutal power of
capitalism. Militarism cripples our activity ; it is the
storm in the preceding sultriness of which our Party
life becomes sluggish and parliamentarianism is being
overtaken and hampered more and more by langour.

Weakening militarism means furthering the possibilities of a further peaceful organic development or,
at least, limiting the possibilities of violent collisions ;
it further means, above all, the infusion of fresh life and
vigour into the political life and the Party struggle.
As a result of a ruthless and systematic fight against
militarism the Party becomes strengthened and impreg-
nated with the revolutionary spirit ; it is the source
which invigorates the revolutionary spirit.

From all this follows the necessity of not only fighting
militarism, but of fighting it in a special manner. Such
a dangerous structure with so many ramifications can
only be dealt with by action which is strong, bold and
on a large scale, and has as many ramifications, action
which tirelessly pursues militarism into all its nooks and
corners, being *toujours en vedette*. The dangerousness
of the fight against militarism also compels one to take
special action which is more elastic and more capable
of adapting itself to circumstances than agitation of a
general kind. However much people in Germany have
striven and still strive against this conception, the
following facts need but be pointed out to overcome all
reluctance and to dispel all doubts and misgivings : we
have a special propaganda for women and young people ;
not only have we specialized the agitation amongst
agricultural workers, but also the Trade Union propa-

ganda inside individual crafts; finally, we may point out the successful anti-militarist propaganda conducted in other countries. It is probably a question of a very short time before the fundamental idea of the motion 114 rejected at Mannheim becomes generally recognized. *This kind of action has also been made the duty of German Social-Democracy by the well-known unanimous decision of the International Congress of* 1900.

The demand for such special propaganda has absolutely nothing to do with the un-historical Anarchist conception of militarism. We are conscious in the clearest possible way of the *rôle* which militarism plays under capitalism; and, of course, we have not the remotest idea of setting militarism above capitalism or on a level with it because it constitutes only a part of capitalism. It is, more correctly speaking, a specially pernicious and dangerous life manifestation of capitalism. Our whole agitation against capitalism is directed against the life manifestations of capitalism in which it assumes concrete shape. We can indicate the domain of the anti-militarist fight to a certain extent as something apart from the general political struggle, something alongside the Trade Union struggle or even alongside the co-operative and educational struggle, if you will. In other words, we are anti-militarists as anti-capitalists.*

If anti-militarism has historically grown everywhere out of generalities of rather a theoretical nature into an important and effective practical movement, hand in hand with the employment of troops in civil war, against the enemy at home, this, of course, does not furnish a single weighty reason against a special anti-militarist propaganda being started in the countries in which, so far, such employment of troops has been practically avoided, or has taken place so far back that it has disappeared from the consciousness of the people. It has always been the pride of Social-Democracy not to become afraid of the fire after having been burnt; on the contrary, to learn from history, from sociology and

---

* Further reasons for the need of special anti-militarist propaganda are given on p. 165 and following.

from the experiences of kindred parties to look far into the future, and profiting by such experience to build far in advance. History, sociology and this experience speak in a truly plain manner as regards anti-militarism. And the time is ripe.

CHAPTER VI.

ANTI-MILITARISM IN GERMANY AND THE GERMAN SOCIAL-DEMOCRACY.

THE programme of German Social-Democracy and that of international Socialism, at least, of the Marxist school, sets as its object " The conquest of political power," that is to say, abolition of the social correlation of power of the capitalist oligarchy *versus* the proletariat, and the provisional substitution for it of a democratic proletarian correlation of power ; and this includes, in the first place, the abolition of capitalist militarism, this most important piece of capitalist oligarchic power.

The minimum programme deals with the question of militarism in a special manner, and determines the special problem and special aims in regard to militarism, thus meeting all objections *in principle* to a special anti-militarist propaganda. It demands : " Universal training to bear arms. A citizen army in place of a standing army. Decision on war and peace by the representatives of the people. Settlement of all international disputes by arbitration." Thereby the programme repudiates the unmistakably Utopian standpoint as regards the present and the near future, which is directed not only against militarism, but against every kind of preparation for war ; which repudiates in principle participation not only in wars provoked by capitalism, by political and national reaction, but participation in any war ; which not only fights against war, but also tries to deny in a fantastic manner the actual possibilities of war and the consequences which flow therefrom. So that German Social-Democracy, like the overwhelming majority of all the foreign parties,

even the French party, is not anti-patriotic in the sense
of Hervé or anti-national (Kropotkin), but is non-
patriotic in accordance with the consequence which
flows from its class war character.

It is taken as a matter of course and is disputed by
no one that as a proletarian Party Social-Democracy is
the *unconditional* enemy, the enemy *sans phrase*, the
enemy to the knife of militarism at home ; to tear it out
root and branch is one of its most important tasks.

What has been done in Germany so far to carry out
the decision of the Paris Congress of 1900 ?

The influential leaders of Social-Democracy have
repeatedly resisted the attempt to start a special anti-
militarist propaganda in Germany, by saying that there
is no Social-Democratic Party in the whole world which
fights militarism so much as German Social-Democracy.
There is much truth in this. Ever since the existence
of the German Empire a ruthless criticism has been
incessantly levelled by German Social-Democracy at
militarism, its whole contents and all its abuses, in
Parliament and in the Press. Social-Democracy has
collected a huge mass of material which indicts militarism, and has waged the struggle against militarism
as part of the general agitation with persistent tenacity.
In this respect our Party needs neither defence nor
praise, its deeds speak for it. And yet that which has
taken place on an extensive scale must be supplemented.
We do not at all deny that the anti-militarist fight
which has hitherto been waged has been successful and
that the form of this struggle has corresponded to the
aim pursued ; and we do not dispute that this kind of
struggle will be absolutely indispensable, highly useful
and successful in the future. Yet this does not settle
the question. We must not overlook the question of
the education of the young people, which is the most
essential part of anti-militarist propaganda.

Of course, our general agitation opens people's eyes
and every anti-capitalist and every Social-Democrat
per se is a first-rate anti-militarist, who is most reliable ;
and the anti-militarist bias of our general work of

enlightenment does away with all doubt in this respect. Yet to whom does our general agitation appeal? It is rightly and necessarily cut to the measure of the adult worker, man and woman. However, we do not wish to capture only the adult proletarians, but also the proletarian children, the proletarian young people. . . . "He who has the youth has the future."

Here the remark will be made: He who has the parents has the children of these parents, has the young people! At all events, he would be a miserable Social-Democrat who would not instil into his children the Social-Democratic spirit according to his ability, and bring them up as Social-Democrats. It also coincides with our opinion that the influence of the parents (conjointly with the influence of economic, social and political conditions under which the proletarian youth grows up and which, though constituting the most important and at the same time the most obvious means of agitation and enlightenment, cannot be influenced by the Party activity and have to be disregarded on principle) can easily defeat all attempts on the part of reaction and capitalism to capture the children's minds in a cunning manner. But the subject cannot be dismissed with this argument. It is precisely a clear examination of the above trend of thought which shows wherein our present agitation fails, and fails continuously in an ever greater degree and calls for a solution in a pressing manner.

"Every Social-Democrat brings up his children as Social-Democrats," but only to the best of his ability. This is the first serious shortcoming. How many people do generally understand the work of education, even given time and goodwill, and how many Social-Democratic proletarians, even when they have the best will, have the necessary time for education, and how many have the necessary knowledge? In many cases the women and other members of the family who are backward in their enlightenment unfortunately far outweigh any possible educational influence that a class-conscious father might exert. If the Party wishes to do its duty

it must be ready to help with education in the home by
striving after educating the young people in a general
way and by carrying on a special agitation amongst the
young people in particular, which must necessarily have
an anti-militarist bias.

And further, how many proletarians are really enlightened Social-Democrats? Enlightened to such an
extent that they themselves can enlighten others in
regard to the principles of Social-Democratic criticism
and of Social-Democratic aspirations? And how many
proletarians are there in times of peace so ready for
sacrifice and so tireless that they are willing to carry on
incessantly, day by day, the hard, laborious work of
education to the best of their ability? And apart from
those who are partially enlightened, some more, some
less, and the lukewarm who comprise an enormous
number : what a huge number of proletarians are still
complete strangers to Social-Democracy ! Here is a
tremendous field full of the best proletarian shoots, a
field which it is impossible even to survey and wh)se
cultivation should not be postponed until the backward
portions of the adult proletariat have been won over
to our side. Of course, it is easier to influence the
offspring of enlightened parents, but this does not do
away with the possibility and the duty of setting to
work upon the more difficult portion of the proletarian
youth.

Thus the necessity for agitation amongst the young
people is put beyond all doubt, and as this agitation,
in accordance with its object, must work with fundamentally different methods—in harmony with the
different conditions of life, different understanding,
different inclinations and the different character of the
young people—the inference follows that it must be
specialized, that it must be given a special part alongside
the general agitation, and that it is well advised to put
it into the hands of special organs, at least, to a certain
extent. Our agitation (what with the problems facing
the Party, and the decisive struggles drawing ever
nearer) has become so extensive and has so many

ramifications that the necessity for a division of labour is being forced upon it more and more, a division of labour whose relative, but only its relative, difficulties we do not at all ignore.

And now a step still further. Anti-militarist agitation fills quite a special and peculiar *rôle* inside the agitation amongst the young people. It has to appeal to circles which are often inaccessible to the Social Democratic attempts to educate the young people ; it has to stretch out far, much further than do the general efforts at education, to take in those portions of the proletarian young people, which cannot be induced to frequent the workers' educational establishments, courses of instruction, courses of lectures, and cannot be induced to read regularly the general literature for young people. The anti-militarist agitation has also to appeal to the young proletarians who as they grow older, hardly come in contact with the general efforts at education. Yes, its proper domain is the young people from 17 to 21 years of age. It has a far more propagandist character than the general efforts at education. The forms of this agitation have to depart from the forms of the latter, at least to a certain extent. Also, owing to its special dangerousness, it would be better not to couple it with those strivings of a general kind : on the one hand, in order not to render these general strivings more difficult than is absolutely necessary and not bring discredit upon them, on the other hand, to take steps to avoid the dangers besetting the anti-militarist agitation as far as possible by putting it under the guidance of specially instructed persons who are familiar with all the pitfalls. And, finally, the anti-militarist material (to wit, ill-treatment of soldiers, military justice, etc.) is so enormous and so scattered that even here a division of labour and specialization are necessary simply in order to make the best possible use of it all ; and not only to make use of it, but also to compile, sift and put it into shape.

It is precisely the last argument which shows that anti-militarist agitation, even amongst adults, can become more effective through being specialized.

Thus there is ample opportunity for work which will bring its reward!

And what success has been so far achieved in regard to developing anti-militarism by means of the kind of anti-militarist agitation hitherto employed in Germany?

Certainly a large part of the German army is already "red." A mere glance at the Party groupings within the German nation shows this to be the case. And this fact which is taken as a matter of course is the reason that induced the famous chief of the "Imperial Union," Lieutenant-General von Liebert, to take up the pen to write the amusing, much talked of book, "The Development of Social-Democracy and Its Influence on the German Army" (now held in contempt because of its helplessness even by Max Lorenz, the Social-Democratic renegade, who, in accordance with his profession, now burns that of which he used to be a devotee), and has induced General von Eichhorn to introduce anti-Social-Democratic instruction (in the army) in the autumn of 1906. Certainly, nearly one-third of the German electors, that is to say of the male German subjects over 25 years of age, voted for Social-Democracy in the Reichstag elections of 1903 ; of course, it may also be true in a general way, at least for the time being, that Social-Democracy has a stronger following among the younger " classes " than amongst the older " classes." But for all that it is doubtful whether this proportion already holds good in regard to the " classes " of 21-22 years ; it also must be quite plain to us that these young men generally do not at all belong to the elements which are firm in their convictions, and that there is a tremendous difference between casting a vote for Social-Democracy or really being a Social-Democrat, or even being ready to face all the personal dangers which follow in the wake of anti-militarism in the army. Even though " psychology," " suggestion," the " logic of blood," which have been dealt with elsewhere, may be powerful contributory agents in demoralizing discipline, there can be no question of even one-third of the army approximately being in such a spiritual and moral frame

of mind as would render impossible or, at least, difficult
its employment in a violent unconstitutional action, in
a *coup d'état*, against the enemy at home, against the
Labour movement.

It is true that matters are more unfavourable to
militarism in the case of mobilizing the reserve and the
landwehr, especially for war. In October, 1906, a
military collaborator of *Vorwaerts* pointed out that
amongst the reservists and the men of the *landwehr*
called up in the case of war (who would in that case
comprise about four-fifths of the whole army) at least
one million men could still be looked upon as unreliable
in the militarist sense. To be sure, we take up a critical
attitude even in this respect and do not conceal it that
militarist mass " suggestion," also mass psychosis and
the " suggestion " of the militarist authority in command
can even here knock a big hole in the calculation of this
military collaborator.

What is here achieved is achieved by means of the
general propaganda inside the Labour movement.
So far scarcely anything has been done by the propagandist activity of the German Social-Democracy, in
the way of making a special appeal to the future soldiers.
Apart from the well-known " Guide to Those Liable to
Military Service " and from the leaflet issued by the
Party Executive in the summer of 1906 we know of
nothing suitable in this respect ; both these publications
deal exclusively with the legal provisions applicable to
those in the army. True though it is that evolution
works for us, it is not true that everything comes about
of its own accord ; true though it is that quietism and
fatalism of this kind are a gross mistake in the sense of
historical materialism, and the grave-diggers of all
agitation, just as true is it that agitation not only of a
general kind but even a special anti-militarist propaganda
is vindicated ; and it is true that anti-militarist propaganda in Germany must be improved quickly and
energetically. To the South German " Young Guards "
is due the credit of having fearlessly tackled the practical
solution of the problem ; to be sure, this is only a small

beginning, but it will, and must, soon find energetic support if for nought else than to nip in the bud the Anarchist anti-militarism which is beginning to make its appearance in Germany.

And we keep asking : " Is German Social-Democracy, the German Labour movement—the nucleus and the *élite* troop of the new International, as it likes to be called—because either over-prudent or over-confident, going to refrain from tackling this problem till, inadequately armed and straining to the utmost all its strength and its methods of fighting, it is faced by the fact of a world war or an intervention* in Russia, which can to a certain extent be avoided and for which German Social-Democracy would also have to bear the responsibility ? "

And, finally, have not the German workers been spurred on sufficiently by the police massacres of workers which also come under the scope of anti-militarist propaganda ?

Be this as it may : German Social-Democracy must not shut its eyes to the fact that to militarism the following words must be applied : *si vis pacem, para bellum !* Make a start with anti-militarist propaganda as early as possible in order to reduce in advance as far as possible the dangerousness of militarism for the proletariat !

And the fact that this kind of propaganda is specially difficult in Germany should really be no reason for its postponement ; on the contrary, it should be a stimulus towards its acceleration.

The time for a move on the part of the German proletariat is ripe enough now, and the general political situation at home under which the German proletariat groans is as desperate as need be.

---

* The improbability of such a contingency is beyond all doubt ; but it has not become less improbable in consequence of Prince Buelow's declaration in the German Reichstag on 4th November, 1906,

CHAPTER VII

THE ANTI-MILITARIST TASKS OF THE GERMAN SOCIAL-DEMOCRACY.

ANTI-PATRIOTIC anti-militarism has found and will find no suitable soil in Germany. But the propaganda of German Social-Democracy will have to be permeated to an ever greater degree with the propagation of the international solidarity of Labour and with the propagation of the peace of nations as an aim of the proletarian struggle of liberation. The demands of the anti-militarist programme discussed above form a suitable basis to which no objection can be raised.

Generally speaking, militarism at home and all its perniciousness—more felt in normal times—with its many ramifications will have to contend with ever greater difficulties and thus the class-war character of militarism will become more prominent. Where the main attack is to be launched will be decided at the time by the national and international situation.

Whatever forms and whatever methods of propaganda we have to perfect or introduce in Germany—and we have to assume as a matter of course that we shall have to keep within legal limits—the question of doing propaganda inside the army has to be rejected in advance.

German Social-Democracy has not even done enough in regard to collecting the material which indicts militarism. Only the military budget, the growth of the indirect military burdens, and the peace footing of the army, have been frequently set out in more detail. The connection between the military burdens and the protective and the taxation policies also awaits a closer examination. And what, above all, is lacking is an account of the ill-treatment of soldiers, of the exploits of military justice, of suicides amongst soldiers, of conditions of hygiene in the army, injuries caused while on service, of conditions of pay and pensions as well as an account of the employment of soldiers in forcing down wages and of the decrees of the army corps relating thereto, an account of the employment of soldiers, and of soldiers about to be disbanded, as strike-breakers, further, of the intervention by the military and armed police in strikes, of the victims who have succumbed as a result of such action, an account of the system of military boycott, military intervention in cases of political action, an account of making use of the military societies in the socio-political and political struggle, further of the exploits of militarism in all these domains in other countries especially in the economic and the political struggle ; in which case a special account is to be opened for militarism, navalism, and colonial militarism. We have insufficient knowledge of the material relating to the militarist Young People's societies of our opponents, and of the material which relates to the anti-militarist movement and to the manner in which it is opposed, nor has it been put into proper order.

The regular collection, sifting and collation of all this material must be systematically taken in hand ; it is impossible to treat it as a side-issue in connection with the general agitation.

Of course, this material would have to be used first in the general agitation, in parliament and in the press, in leaflets of a general kind and at meetings. But it must be directed to definite objectives and into definite channels in order to permeate and render fertile those strata of the population which are specially important for anti-militarism. First of all we have to consider the question not only of the youths liable to military service, but also the parents, especially the mothers, who should be specially mobilized for educating the young people in anti-militarism ; also the question of the older workers whose influence upon the young workers and apprentices should be made use of as much as possible in this direction. And, finally, the struggle against the Military Societies should be carried on in a more vigorous and regular way.

The agitation will not be able to call anywhere directly or indirectly for military disobedience, but it will have attained its aim completely if it creates clearness about the essence of militarism and its *rôle* in the class struggle, and if it rouses indignation and loathing against militarism by effectively bringing to the fore its qualities and deeds antagonistic to the people.

Where the laws permit it the Young Socialist organizations will have to be the chief bearers of this propaganda which, without doubt, undermines militarism or militarist sentiments by fostering class-consciousness. The Young Socialist societies will have to spread the anti-militarist spirit more and more in a form suited to the understanding of young people by means of pamphlets, leaflets, lectures, courses of lectures and by instruction. Festivities and artistic entertainments will have to be made use of for the same end. Again, the members of the societies will have to be educated as propagandists of anti-militarism. By agitation by word of mouth amongst their class-mates of the same age, by spreading their literature the members of the Young Socialist organizations will turn their families, relations and friends, the workshop and the factory into a recruiting ground.

The Young Socialist organization itself must not limit its agitation to its members, but extend it as far as possible. It should appeal to the whole mass of the young workers. It must also attract the older workers in the manner described above. It must work systematically through the medium of the press, leaflets, pamphlets, general meetings, public lectures, artistic entertainments, festivities and so on, which are to be arranged both for the young people generally as well as for adults who are to be won over by the anti-militarist Young Socialist agitation. Giving send-offs to recruits and demonstrations of every kind (where permitted) must serve the same purpose.

In addition the Party must, as hitherto, in an ever greater degree systematically take up the question of the soldiers and non-commissioned officers, must represent energetically their material and social* interests in parliament, and thus try to win the sympathies of these circles in a way which cannot be legally taken exception to.

The foundation of special societies of ex-soldiers after the fashion of the Belgian and Dutch societies with the special task of opposing the Military Societies is not to be recommended for Germany : the general political and Trade Union organizations suffice here.

If we look around at what has taken place in other countries we see how much more remains for us to do ; and if we scan the above programme we notice that the Party, much though it may have done in the domain of anti-militarism, has only just made a beginning in the fulfilment of its duty ; to a certain extent it is in its infancy as regards anti-militarist propaganda.

That all these many-sided tasks cannot be tackled from a centre at present is obvious, as is also the fact that we must make it our future aim to direct and control them from a centre. The establishment of a central committee for this purpose appears as a matter of necessity, because only in this way can we make sure that all lawful possibilities of agitation are made use of while observing due caution. Anti-militarist propaganda must be cast over the whole nation like a wide net. The proletarian youth must be systematically imbued with class-consciousness and with hatred of militarism. This kind of agitation would warm the hearts and rouse the youthful enthusiasm of the young proletarians. The proletarian youth belongs to Social-Democracy, to Social-Democratic anti-militarism. It must, and will, be won over if everyone does his duty. *He who has the youth has the army.*

THE END.

---

* Improving the conditions of pay, of food, clothing, quarters, treatment, and rendering the service less arduous, fighting against ill-treatment, reforming the law concerning discipline, punishment, lodging complaints, military justice, etc.